Anonymous

Amherst

Alpha delta phi

Anonymous

Amherst
Alpha delta phi

ISBN/EAN: 9783337090913

Printed in Europe, USA, Canada, Australia, Japan

Cover: Foto ©ninafisch / pixelio.de

More available books at **www.hansebooks.com**

1837–18

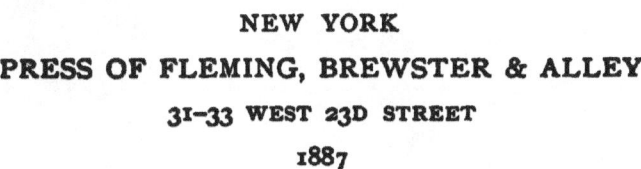

NEW YORK
PRESS OF FLEMING, BREWSTER & ALLEY
31–33 WEST 23D STREET
1887

COMMITTEE OF ARRANGEMENTS FOR THE SEMI-CENTENNIAL CELEBRATION.

JOHN ELLIOTT SANFORD, '51.
WILLIAM HAYES WARD, '56.
FRANCIS DRAPER LEWIS, '69.
E. WINCHESTER DONALD, '69.
HENRY B. RICHARDSON, '69.
TALCOTT WILLIAMS, '73.
ALFRED ELY, '74.
JOSEPH CONVERSE GRAY, '76.
FRANK LUSK BABBOTT, '78.
CHARLES M. PRATT, '79.
B. W. HITCHCOCK, '81.
AND. PORTER ALVORD, '87.
WILLIAM TYLER BLISS, '87.
HOWARD OGDEN WOOD, '87.

EDITORS OF THE MEMORIAL VOLUME.

TALCOTT WILLIAMS, '73.
HENRY C. FOLGER, JR., '79.

PUBLIC EXERCISES

COLLEGE HALL, TUESDAY A.M., JUNE 28, 1887,

10.30 O'CLOCK

MUSIC

PRAYER

THE REV. MICHAEL BURNHAM, D.D., '67.

MUSIC

INTRODUCTORY ADDRESS

THE RT. REV. FREDERIC DAN HUNTINGTON, D.D., LL.D., '39.

COMMEMORATIVE ADDRESS

THE REV. RICHARD SALTER STORRS, D.D., LL.D., '39.

MUSIC

BANQUET

PRATT GYMNASIUM, TUESDAY P.M., JUNE 28, 1887,

9 O'CLOCK

INTRODUCTORY REMARKS BY THE TOASTMASTER.
  HON. JOHN E. SANFORD, '51.

THE RELATION OF GREEK LETTER SOCIETIES TO COLLEGE DISCIPLINE.
  PRESIDENT JULIUS H. SEELYE.

A HALF CENTURY AGO.
  REV. E. E. BLISS, D.D., '37.

THE CHIVALRY OF $\Alpha\Delta\Phi$.
  HON. ALGERNON S. SULLIVAN, *Miami*, '45.

Α Δ Φ IN THE PULPIT.
> REV. E. K. ALDEN, D.D., '44.

Α Δ Φ IN POLITICS.
HON. GEORGE WILLIAM CURTIS, *Brunonian*, '54.

FIFTY YEARS OF AMERICAN SCHOLARSHIP.
REV. WILLIAM HAYES WARD, D.D., LL.D.,'56.

THE FRATERNITY OF *Α Δ Φ*.
> HON. JOSEPH H. CHOATE, *Harvard*, '52.

GREEK LETTERS AND LETTERS LITERARY.
> PROF. F. A. MARCH, '45.

BROTHERHOOD WITHIN AND WITHOUT.
HON. H. S. STOCKBRIDGE, '45.

LOVE THE SISTERHOOD.
> PRESIDENT T. J. BACKUS, *Rochester*, '64.

*THE LAW AND THE CHAPTER.
> HON. F. W. ROCKWELL, '68.

*HENRY WARD BEECHER AND ROSWELL D. HITCHCOCK, *Sons of Amherst and of Α Δ Φ*.
> REV. E. W. DONALD, D.D., '69.

*THE CHAPTER AS IT IS.
> E. C. HUNTINGTON, '88.

*THE PAST AND FUTURE OF THE CHAPTER.
> PROF. H. H. NEILL, '66.

*OUR SISTER CHAPTERS.
> F. L. STETSON, *Williams*, '67.
> E. M. SHEPARD, *Manhattan*, '69.

---

* Owing to the lateness of the hour, these toasts were not called for.

PUBLIC EXERCISES

INTRODUCTORY ADDRESS.

THE RT. REV. FREDERIC DAN HUNTINGTON, D.D., LL.D., '39.

The Amherst Chapter of the Alpha Delta Phi, celebrating with joy its semi-centennial, has inquired which one of its strong brotherhood ought to be its spokesman. Studying the catalogue of names, now nearly four hundred, representing most of the departments of learning and action in American society—many of them eminent, and all of them, we believe, honorable—going from the bottom to the top, and from the top to the bottom, has fixed with confidence upon the name of Richard Salter Storrs. No man and no woman who has heard his voice needs to be bidden to listen while he speaks.

I count it a special personal privilege and pleasure to introduce the orator of the day, my classmate and my friend, the Pastor of the Church of the Pilgrims.

THE BROADER RANGE AND OUTLOOK OF MODERN COLLEGE TRAINING.

RICHARD S. STORRS, D.D., LL.D., '39.

Mr. President, Brothers of Alpha Delta Phi, Ladies and Gentlemen:

An institution like this, whose annual commencement attracts and greets us, has its peculiar indwelling life, which ever freshly reveals itself through the constant impulse to expansion and growth. Departments of study are added one by one to those which had preceded, while each of those before established seeks to afford wider instruction, with more exact training; new teachers are added, more fit and adequate apparatus of instruction is diligently sought and considerately supplied, and the whole scheme of study becomes more practical and more generous, aiming to meet continually wider and finer needs, and to furnish to prepared and inquisitive minds a completer supply of what they seek of training and of truth. This is the law of such institutions, only in fulfilling which do they show themselves worthy of honor or of maintenance; in the absence of cordial obedience to which they become inevitably, after a little, groups of sparsely occupied buildings covering acres which the plough might more usefully traverse. The vigor, abundance and fruitfulness of the life of any college are manifested and measured by the changes which progressively take place in the courses and methods of its instruction, and in the physical structures and instruments through which it imparts this. Therefore it always needs liberal friends, and an ampler endowment; and the time never comes when it can say that its desires are answered, its equipment is complete.

It is not, therefore, an occasion of surprise when we return here to find that enlargements and alterations, manifold and conspicuous, have taken place in our absence; and if we look back, as some of us to-day do, over a term of fifty years since the infant chapter of our fraternity found here its incipient life and early cradle, we expect to discover, upon recalling that long-ago, that the changes accomplished and still going on have made almost another college of that with which we were familiar. The same skies are above us, effulgent in the dawn with sunrise lights which we used to see or shiveringly to watch for at six in the morning, resplendent at sunset with a glory which none of us has seen surpassed, amid whatever ethereal charm or purple glow of Italy itself. The same landscape is before us, rimmed with hills, but stretching far outward toward the west, now rich with verdure, blazing in autumn in the vast vestment of many colors, while always lovely in its modulated lines, with the reflected flash of waters touching it at points with sparkling shimmer. Some of the same buildings are here, tarrying, perhaps, beyond what those who have to use them conceive the fitness of things to require, but connecting the college as now presented, through somewhat rude and rusty links, with the college as it was, while making us all glad to know that the law of progress, elsewhere so effective, has undergone no final suspense before their ancient and homely walls; and the same village, though far more beautiful, is around us now that was here when as boys we trod these streets, were lodged, perhaps, in some of these houses, strolled over these fields, or took, it may be, our private spin — very private! — behind whatever horses could be hired, on the neighboring roads.

These remain; but in almost everything which directly pertains to the college, the scene is one of transformation. One professor continues here—long may he continue!—under whom some of us ploughed our way through parts of Livy, or grappled the condensed martial sentences, with the tone of tragic battle in them, of the great master Tacitus, or caught some swift and inspiriting glimpse of Attic philosophy, eloquence, poetry, story. All the others have passed from the scenes in which they were to us at the time illustrious persons, and their places are filled by others. Different buildings, another chapel, a new library, a new observatory, a new and splendid gymnasium are before us; and the physical apparatus of instruction is widely diverse from that with which those of us who have passed our threescore years, and are rapidly completing the supplementary ten, were formerly familiar. The change has not been startlingly rapid in its particulars, but it has been persistent, continuous, general, and we may hope that it has been prophetic; that other changes are to follow, as needful as these, and yet more wide. It is a fact always impressive, and one which lifts our thoughts forward with spontaneous impulse on an occasion like this, that such an institution counts scores of years as in personal life we count the months; that classes coming and classes going are but recurring incidents in its history, and that to its incorporeal life the century is not long.

The most significant change of all which we observe has been in the broader scope and the fresh elasticity given to the courses of study pursued here, with the more various and large opportunity systematically offered for a more comprehensive and elaborate training than in our time was proposed or was possible. The college remains a college for training, not aspiring to become a university, which in its intent represents a universal cyclopædia of knowledge, housed in libraries, but supposed to be also vitally incorporate, and the more accessible because peripatetic, in a multitude of teachers. Such an institution has, beyond question, important advantages; but this is not such an one. Its purpose is, as it was at the beginning, to discipline men in the use of their powers, while opening to them inviting opportunities for profitable study, in large part now along lines of inquiry which they select. But the variety of these lines of study is far more abundant and attractive than it was, and the developing life of the college has been shown in this direction almost more distinctly than in any other.

When some of us were here as students, a half century ago, the courses of training were all arranged with reference to the professional studies, in law or medicine, or especially in theology, which it was implicitly assumed were to follow. Even as so planned and maintained they were meagre, restricted, sharply mandatory. We had, of course, Latin and Greek, grammatically taught, till some of us wished that republican Rome had never existed, and that the Persians had conquered

Greece. We had mathematics, which to many were a weariness to spirit and mind, as well as to the flesh. We had more or less of natural science, as then understood; something of philosophy, with dear Dr. Brown's mellifluous lectures on the human mind for our principal text-book; something, no doubt, of instruction in ethics, though I cannot remember what author was expected to serve as our enlightening guide and friend. We had moderate courses in rhetoric and logic, and a very slight smattering of French. Besides these, I do not remember anything of importance in the field of survey opened to us. We had no German, Italian or Spanish; no history; very little, if anything, of political economy; no instruction in art; no leadership into the life of the Old World and the secrets of its renown, and no elective studies whatever. The grooves were definite and constrictive, and we were to move along them as we might, looking out at the end, as I have suggested, on one or other of the three professions toward which the college was to open the way.

From that to this the change is apparent, of large reach, and of radical importance.

Now I observe that German, French, Italian, Spanish are systematically taught; that opportunity is offered for an initial study of Sanskrit—that prolific otherworld matrix from which the whole family of the languages popularly known as Indo-European trace their descent; that English literature and the English language, back to the Anglo-Saxon times, have prominent places in the curriculum; that philosophy, both intellectual and moral, is far more extensively and profoundly expounded; that biology takes its place with geology and chemistry; that the recent art collections—presenting copies of statues and groups of sculpture from the best Greek and Roman periods, of the frieze of the Parthenon, of the Olympian Hermes and Victory, of the bronze Gates of Ghiberti, "worthy to be the gates of Paradise"—become the occasion for illustrative lectures; that the life and literature of the magnificent ancient peoples are set forth in picturesque portraiture for those who seek to master their languages; that the great mediæval Latin hymns are brought under appreciative review; best of all, perhaps, that the library, which in our time was a place for preserving, in security, no doubt, but in utter secrecy, any book which had drifted into it from a clergyman's shelves, now contains nearly fifty thousand volumes, most of them freshly selected, in all departments of study, and is still steadily increasing. Meantime, the new and superb gymnasium gives opportunity and constant incentive to a graceful and finished physical culture ; and history appears, the true preserver and mistress of knowledges, established in a principal place among elective studies from the beginning of the junior year onward.

No one, I am sure, will question the wisdom of changes like these, or will fail to be grateful for the successive gifts and endowments which have rendered them possible, as no one, either, can fail to see to what a vastly widened outlook for the effect of college-training such changes and expansions point. Where it was the rigorous aim to train men for one of the three professions then called "learned," the object now evidently is to give the more liberal, many-sided instruction, which shall fit men for useful, happy and illuminated lives, in any department of future activity, professional, educational, editorial, artistic, or commercial, social and domestic. To accustom men to right methods of study, and to form in them the habit of pursuing such methods, thus starting them fairly on their courses of independent inquiry, while giving them just and liberal views of the changing thought and life of the world, that they may be more cultivated persons wherever afterward they may live, and whatever work they may accept—this is now the purpose of the college. It is a wise and beautiful purpose, which must command the approval of all. In a constantly increasing multitude of persons, throughout widening circles, life will be silently but generously enriched by the studies here pursued. In all walks of life, and not only in the professions, those will appear who feel themselves owing a debt of gratitude to the text-books and the teachers from whom they received early guidance with an energetic and continuing impulse.

Let me illustrate this somewhat more distinctly, by noticing the peculiar and permanent benefits of that study of history which, as I said, was here formerly wholly ignored, but which now has a place so prominent and constant sympathetically assigned to it. This special instance will, perhaps, present as clearly as any, both the extent and the benefit of the change which has here taken place.

Of course the recorded annals of mankind cannot be exhibited, can hardly be sketched in more than vague outline, by the most accomplished and diligent teacher, in the term of two years. But the great periods in history can be distinguished; the places of some eminent persons in its inter-connected though complex development can be fairly indicated, and the general trend of the forces which it shows, in particular ages or in the whole far-spreading progress, can be clearly set forth. What is better still, those who enter on the study can have their taste for it cherished, can learn the rewarding methods of inquiry, can be assisted to a fairly critical judgment of authors, and be distinctly set upon the path toward wider, finer and more exact knowledge to be subsequently gained; and these are effects important in themselves, while alive with promise, which will make any two years of study of memorable value.

The mind is always expanded and liberalized by what puts distant lands and times, with the exacting and disciplinary experiences of one's own ancestors or of other peoples, distinctly before it. To a certain extent foreign travel does this, as it sets the immeasurably wider expanses, filled with energetic and laborious life, in contrast with the narrower scenes with which one before had been familiar; and he who has stood with any thoughtfulness amid the crowded immensities of London—an empire in itself, who has looked through curious whirls of reminiscence upon the ancient streets of Paris or its stately boulevards, or who has followed the Unter den Linden from the Schloss to the Brandenburg Gate, before whom Munich, Vienna, Venice, Florence, Naples, Milan, Madrid, have opened their treasures, to whom Rome has appeared, across the Campagna, a city ascending out of the past, but with the dome of later date roofing the throne of its existing empire of souls—such a man can never again be in mind, in range of thought, in intellectual sympathy, what he was before the broadening experience. It is thus that the easier modern modes of foreign travel become educational, and that those are multiplying in all our communities who have been essentially widened in view, by their acquaintance with other lands, for the contemplation of proximate questions. The parish period has almost disappeared from even our popular mental development.

But history, when carefully studied—studied as it should be, with maps, topographic plans, careful itineraries, photographs of monuments or of sites—does the same thing for the home-keeping student, and does it in some important respects in a yet freer and bolder fashion. Egypt, Greece, Assyria, Persia, the scanty and rugged strip of Palestine from which influences have come to regenerate the world, India, China, the vast outstretch of Russia, from lands of the olive and the fig, the pomegranate and the palm, to the lands of the frozen mammoth and the midnight sun—we may not traverse these in our journeying, unless we give our life to the business, but they come before us in the intelligent study of history, in panoramic breadth, with photographic distinctness. The centuries of the past present themselves in perspective. We see the vast cosmical movements from which states have been born, in which subsequent civilizations took rise, and in which the devout mind discovers silent procedures of Providence. We learn how far removed from us were initial influences that are now flowering into results, and how our life is affected at this hour by political combinations and military collisions which preceded by ages the invasion of England by the Normans or the splendid schemes of Charlemagne.

It is quite impossible that one who reads with comprehensive attention, till this immense and vital picture is in a measure opened before him, should not be consciously broadened in thought, expanded even in mental power; that he should not freshly and deeply feel how limited is his individual sphere; how local, although multiplied by endowments from the past, are his personal opportunities; what a vast scheme it is which is being evolved through stir of discussion, rush of emigration, competitions of industries, crash of conflict, by the power which gives its unity to history, and which is perpetually educing great harmonies out of whatever seeming discords. An influence of the same kind descends upon one in the review of geologic periods, or in the contemplation of that stupendous celestial architecture which shows the infinitesimal minuteness of the spinning globe on which we live. But the influence of the study of historical life, crowning the planet with the mystery and majesty of personal forces in long career, makes always a keener appeal to our consciousness, while it inevitably associates itself, by natural impulse, with those sublime scientific speculations which trace the fire-mist as it rounds into a world, and which show the universe, in the immeasurable co-ordination of its physical forms under the rule of harmonious laws, a house of beauty for beautiful souls.

Not merely a general expansion of thought, and, one may say, of the compass of the mind, comes with this larger study of history. It trains directly, with vigorous force, in fine proportion, each chief intellectual faculty. In this respect it is often misconceived by those who regard it as a pleasant exercise, to be pursued at one's leisure, but not to be reckoned on as imparting to the mind elastic vigor, any fresh robustness and alertness of power, or any refined capacity of perceptive insight. Of course the memory will be trained, perhaps all will admit, by the effort to hold distant periods and persons distinctly in view; to keep epochs, and the movements which marked them, from becoming confused and entangled in thought; and to recall, without reference to books, the points at which tendencies affecting subsequent centuries slowly or suddenly became apparent, or at which important tributary influences came in to reinforce them. But beyond the memory, it often is doubted if history offers any energetic or symmetrical discipline to the mind which pursues it. On the other hand, it seems too evident to be questioned that the vigilant, analytic, and reconciling judgment, by which we separate things that differ, and harmonize and associate things that agree, however unlike in outward show; by which we extricate the governing forces beneath phenomena, and set in their historic synthesis the individual designs and the public aspirations which co-operate in movements of general importance—that this noble power is essentially trained, as it is certainly constantly exercised, in any true study of history. I think that many present will agree that for themselves no other form of mental practice has had closer relation to such an intimate and enduring effect; and I am quite satisfied that in either of the professions, in journalism, in educational work, or in the simply private life of an educated citizen, this effect will appear; that one accustomed to wide and searching historical inquiries will be more expert in judging of urgent practical questions presented to-day, and will have a more discerning apprehension of the forces working to modify legislation and to mould society—forces which are often more formidable, or more replete with victorious energy, because subtle and occult.

It seems to me plain, too, that the intuitive moral reason to which the most conspicuous action must give its account, and by which its character is interpreted and adjudged, which puts a candid estimate upon motives, and sets whatever historic achievement presents itself for review in fair connection with special environments of time or of place, must here find as fruitful activity, as systematic and quickening a nurture, as in any department of human research ; and that the historical imagination—which of course does not rank with the creative imagination of the poet, but which is surely akin to that, and perhaps not less capable of giving incitement and beautiful pleasure in common experience—that this has such impulse and sustenance in the study of the past as cannot be furnished anywhere else. So it is that many of the aspiring and superior minds which have wrought in letters have taken this study for their own, and have by their successes in it made the world of readers their grateful debtors. The "personal equation" has continually appeared among them, in their judgment of motives, of movements, and of men ; but in order to form any judgment at all, which the discerning would respect, they have had to cultivate moral insight, as well as a discursive and commanding intelligence. Records of the centuries, buried in the crypts of archives and libraries, have had to yield up to the survey of their genius living forms; vanished times have had to be reconstructed by their thought, in their outward phenomena, and their constitutive moral and social forces ; the manifold sensibilities, desires, passions, which belong to our nature, have had to be recognized, and their operation in public affairs to be patiently exhibited, while the impressions of peoples on each other have filled to the edge the crowded canvas.

No teachers, therefore, have done more than these to educate broadly the ethical and the mental faculty in those whom they addressed, and before whom they unrolled the immense panorama of action, passion, collision, catastrophe, in the story of nations, with the energies exerted at critical points by particular persons, the deeper and more controlling power belonging to tendencies. It is strictly true, what Macaulay said : " He [who reads history] learns to distinguish what is local from what is universal ; what is transitory from what is eternal ; to discriminate between exceptions and rules ; to trace the operation of disturbing causes; to separate the general principles, which are always true and everywhere applicable, from the accidental circumstances with which in every community they are blended, and with which, in an isolated community, they are confounded by the most philosophical mind. Hence it is that in generalization the writers of modern times have far surpassed those of antiquity. The historians of our own country," he adds, "are unequaled in depth and precision of reason ; and even in the works of our mere compilers we often meet with speculations beyond the reach of Thucydides or Tacitus." This is the testimony of one who delighted to tear the vigor and flower of his life from the Bar and the Senate, from official distinction and the rarest social opportunities, that he might survey with ampler scope, while investigating with microscopic minuteness, the records of the past ; reading a week to fashion a sentence ; finding reward for laborious journeys in the more precise outline of a character, or the more exact picture of a scene, in even the more lively turn of a phrase or the more lucid completeness of a paragraph. If one needs to see, in near example, the fitness of historical studies to quicken and maintain high mental enthusiasm, and to discipline and enrich as well as to enlist rare and various mental powers, he may certainly find the immediate demonstration in the instance of Lord Macaulay.

A college like this, too, and an audience like the present, can never fail gratefully to recognize the large and beautiful moral impulse delivered upon spirits prepared to receive it through their contact in history with great, serene and masterful personalities, as these present themselves in the crowded passages which study explores, daring or suffering in the conflicts of their time. In common life we can, at best, but rarely meet such. The saintly and superior souls are not mustered in regiments. Multitudinous companies of elect spirits do not yet surround us on earth. It seems, sometimes, as if the enormous secular advances of which our times are so full and so proud were lowering the height and dimming the lustre of the moral ideal, as represented in the actual of life. Sending messages by lightning, traveling at forty miles to the hour, crossing in a week the ocean which the Mayflower perilously breasted, in our sumptuous vessels, framed of iron, luxurious in appointment, propelled from within, and gay with color as so many swimming summer-gardens — these applauded achievements do not tend of necessity to the upbuilding of nobler courage, to the development of a luminous moral wisdom, to the culture of even philosophical refinement, or the nurture of the temper of devout aspiration. On the other hand, do we not sometimes feel that virtue among us is coming to be too much a matter of manners; that the intense subjective processes from which august character is derived are in a measure being superseded by the mechanical contrivances and the physical successes with which our noisy years resound ; and that the grand and lovely spirits, which are present still, and in which, whensoever we touch them, we find strange charm and inspiration, are fewer and lonelier than they were ? Surely we do not meet them often, and cannot command their presence at our need.

But in history they abound, and are always at our service. Marcus Aurelius, saddest of men, yet imperturbable in a falling empire, and amid the mad whirl of an unexplained universe ; Bernard, with the flaming intensity of his spirit, commander of kings and counselor of pontiffs while the friend and protector of the lowliest of the poor, crushing before him the insolent noble, and facing the fierce fury of the mob on behalf of the Jew ; Melanchthon, with his beautiful enthusiasm for letters, writing Greek more easily than German, modest, peace-loving, yet firm in conviction, devoted to the Master in almost passionate love, the very St. John of the stormy Reformation ; William of Orange, fronting with majestic endurance the apparently irresistible power which swept the Netherlands with flame and blade, and recovering for freedom the land which his ancestors might literally be said to have plucked from the sea—these will come to us when we want them; and with them all, orators, statesmen, theologians, artists leaders of crusades like Godfrey of Bouillon, who would not wear a crown where his Master had borne the cross, rulers of kingdoms like St. Louis, poets, philanthropists, heroes, martyrs, the women with the men, of whom the world of their time was not worthy, by whom the world is made worthier to-day. We may wait years, or we may journey thousands of miles, to meet in the present the special spirit whose office it is, and whose charming prerogative, to kindle and ennoble ours. It is but to step to the library shelf to come face to face with such in the past, if we know where to find them ; nay, it is but to let the thought go backward, over what has become distinct to our minds, and the silent company is around us; the communion of rejoicing and consecrated souls, the illustrious fellowship, in the presence of whom our meanness is rebuked, our cowardice is shamed, and we become the freer children of God and of the Truth.

Not only the romance of the world is in history, but influences so high in source and in force as to be even sacred descend through it. Benedictive, sacramental, is its touch upon responsive souls. We become comparatively careless of circumstances; aware of kinship, in whatever heroic element may be in us, with the choice, transcendent spirits; regardless of the criticism, or the snarling scoffs, which here may surround us, if only conscious of a deeper and more complete correspondence with those whose elate and unsubduable temper remains among the treasures of mankind. I think that to our times, especially, the careful and large study of history is among the most essential sources of moral inspiration. The cultivation of it, in ever larger and richer measure, is one of the finest and noblest exercises proposed to young minds. Any college which introduces to the society of the spirits which have made centuries illustrious, takes splendor and majesty from the office.

The importance of individual life and effort is also magnified by it, instead of being diminished or disguised, as men sometimes fancy; since one is continually reminded afresh of the power which belongs to those spiritual forces which all may assist in animating and moulding civilizations. Of course an imperfect study of history, however rapid and rudimental, shows how often the individual decision and the restraining or inspiring action of great personalities have furnished the pivots on which multitudinous consequences have turned; how, even after long intervals of time, the effects of such have made themselves evident, in changed conditions and tendencies of peoples; and so it reminds us, with incessant iteration, of the vital interlocking of every energetic personal life with the series of lives which are unconsciously dependent upon it, of the reach of its influence upon the great complex of historical progress, and of the service which each capable or eminent spirit may render to the cause of universal culture and peace. But those to whom our thoughts are thus turned have been for the most part signal men in their time, remarkable in power, distinguished in opportunity, intuitively discerning the needs of the age, and with peculiar competence to meet them. With such we by no means may mate ourselves; and, so far, the lesson which history teaches may easily seem to be one of discouragement rather than of impulse, inclining us to rely upon occasional great men as the true pioneers and champions of progress, and to feel that for ourselves we have no place and no responsibility in the assistance of large and permanent public advancement.

But a deeper inquiry shows us at once that such a place and such an obligation belong to each, since each may aid, in the measure of his influence, to establish or renew those spiritual forces which erect and sustain the great and beautiful civilizations. It was, we know, the Hellenic spirit, which not only wreaked itself on immortal expression in the choicest marbles and temples of the world, in the eloquence, the tragedy, the comedy, and the song, the high speculation, and the simple or the stately story, which have for mankind a perennial charm, but which also faced and fought the Persian, and made the names of Marathon and Salamis shine resplendent in the crowded firmament of the world's recollections; only in the decadence of which did Greece yield to the mastery of Macedon. It was the Anglo-Saxon temper which the Norman could not extinguish at Hastings or trample into the bloody ground, which outlived its invaders, conquered its conquerors, and in the end forced them to accept, while modifying in turn, its language, its laws, its popular liberties, and, in great measure, the free spirit of its religion. And it was not, fundamentally, by William or by Maurice—conspicuous as they are on the copious and picturesque pages of Motley—but it was by the spirit, indestructibly regnant among common people, that the otherwise defenseless Batavian plains were saved from the furious ravage of Spain. The men and women who were ready to suffer the loss of all for a King in the heavens—the ministers, by no means accomplished always in the learning of the schools, but who read and expounded the Holy Word in upper rooms, by the light of the flames in which their brethren in faith and in service were being offered as a sacrifice in the resounding squares below —the common sailors who would blow up their ships and find graves in the deep, rather than see the vessels which they manned the prey of their enemies—the promiscuous populations, young and old, nobles and burghers, who would tear away dykes and drown the land, before they would accept for themselves and their children the domination of Philip—these were they who saved their country, giving to their leaders an indomitable power, snatching success from the cruel and haughty hands of what appeared an invincible invasion; and to them, supremely, the world owes the immense augmentation made by that struggle of eighty years to the freedom, prosperity and culture of Europe.

So, after Jena, Prussia was regenerated, under the lead of Von Hardenberg and Von Stein, by the system of common school education; and they, more radically than Bismarck and Von Moltke, have contributed to make that recent kingdom the centre of the German Empire, the arbitrating power in the international politics of Europe. It was true, as the military attaché wrote to his master, the lesser Napoleon, that the schoolmaster, not the needle-gun, triumphed at Sadowa. So Scotland, also, with a comparatively sparse population, on a sterile soil, and under unpropitious skies, has become the seemingly inexhaustible source of great teachings in all departments, industrial, philosophical, theological, poetic. Out of the instructed and invigorated life of the Scottish people have come not only the looms of Paisley, and the vast industries on the Clyde, but Scott and Jeffrey, Erskine and Hume, Chalmers, Guthrie and Hugh Miller, Burns and Carlyle.

Even in the physical world invisible and impalpable forces are those which govern : the light, which strikes without indenting the infant's eye, which no balances can weigh, and whose secret remains undiscovered by man ; the lightning, which subtly paces the wires, and sheds illumination on streets and squares, but which shows its effect, never itself, in the blazing edges of cloven clouds ; the cohesive attractions which build and bind all organized bodies, but which the microscope cannot discern; the life, which no man can analyze or can see except in operation; the inclusive and vast energy of gravitation, which holds at once each pebble on the beach, each flying foam-fleck driven by winds, while it reaches the farthest nebulæ in its grasp, the very muscle of omnipotence compacting the universe in its integrity. Tremendous, immeasurable, as this power is, before its operation no slightest rustle is stirred amid the quiet air. So everywhere, structures decay and forms disappear, the things unseen are the things eternal. It is the same law which manifests itself in national development. Moral forces are always behind the palpable phenomena. The historical progress that moves our admiration has been initiated, and been afterward assured and guided, by spiritual energies. We have never reached the secrets of history till we apprehend these. And every man and every woman has his or her work in the world plainly set forth under the light of this great lesson. It is for each, in the measure of the power and opportunity of each, to cherish and diffuse the temper out of which in their time the great and benign changes shall come. Neither the eloquent and stimulating speech which went before our civil war, nor the military judgment, fortitude, valor, which presided on its historical fields, would have carried to success the vast revolution which we have seen, and for which the country to-day rejoices from the Lakes to the Gulf, except for the patient love of freedom and hatred of slavery which had been nurtured in quiet homes, by peaceful firesides, in the preceding years. In dispersed villages the real battle was fought, not at Gettysburgh or at Shiloh. The splendid burst of our century-plant into a bloom as rich and as brilliant as the continent ever can show, went back to hidden and homely roots. And until that great experience is forgotten, the lesson which all the study of history imperatively teaches cannot lose its emphasis for us: that every one in a civilized and advancing community has the opportunity to do something for the future as well as for the present, and that on each is set the crown of this noble right, and this imperious obligation.

I have no function as preacher here, but I may be permitted to add that history is a department of study leaving, in my judgment, as distinct and salutary religious impressions as does any form of secular knowledge opened to man. Ours is a historical religion; coming to us through historical books, exhibiting its energy through two thousand years, in the recorded advancement of mankind; which may be studied almost as distinctly in the moral and social progress of peoples under its inspiration as in the writings, of narrative and epistle, which represent the source and the government of that progress. Certainly a force incalculable by man was exerted by this religion in the conversion of the Roman Empire from the fierce passions and vices of Paganism to even the partial and qualified acceptance of the pure and austere Christian rule. Make all the allowance which the skeptic can ask for the political and military ambitions which consented to or conspired with the spiritual changes introduced by Christianity, and it still remains an astonishing fact, wholly inexplicable by human analysis, that a recent, unattractive and foreign religion, hated and fought with the utmost fury by those whose only moral alliance was through their common antagonism to it, should in less than three centuries have changed the gardens of Nero into resorts for Christian worship; should have scattered its assemblies and their institutions over the whole civilized world, and have blazoned the cross on the standards of the Empire. It must have had a Divine energy with it and in it to accomplish an effect so strange and stupendous. On any other hypothesis the chances were millions on millions to one, as even thoughtful unbelievers admit, against its success—against, indeed, its continued existence. The astonishing changes wrought by it are to this day almost incredible to those who know what Rome had been under Tiberius, and what it had come to be in the time of Theodosius. A power invisible but also invincible, behind the movement, is as evident as are the subterranean fires in the shining outbreak of volcanoes, or as are the vast subterranean forces beneath the shattering tremble of earthquakes.

Almost equally afterward, in the conquest of barbarian tribes, in the fusion, the restraint and the moral education of the savage, nomadic and relentless populations from which have gradually come into being the Christian states of modern Europe — in the immense constructive energies which silently wrought, but wrought with amazing breadth and effect, amid the mediæval chaos — in the astonishing reformation of religion, opening the Bible to the study of mankind, and using pulpit and printing press for its conquering instruments against majestic establishments of hierarchical power — in the work already in part accomplished upon this continent, and which is swiftly going on in Europe and the East, in India, Africa, the islands of the Pacific — the same celestial, unsubduable energy everywhere confronts us, inhering organically in our religion, while also inseparably associated with it in cosmical operation. No miracle of the Master's time, however fully accredited, shows more distinctly the might of God under the human muscle which it clothed, than do these vast developments in history His intervening thought and will. One sees sometimes in a studio or a gallery a veiled statue, every characteristic line of form and face visible beneath what seems a thin film of lace-work, which itself, however, is wrought in the marble. So the very earth on which we stand is coming to show the face of the Christ, wrought into it from above, and revealed through the reticulated hardness of its slowly yielding civilization. And the mind of Him from whom sprang the genius of the sculptor is supremely declared in this effect.

There is something more, therefore, in the history of Christendom than philosophy teaching by example. It infolds and expresses the Christian Religion, working itself into partial, difficult, but progressive exhibition, through intractable materials, against stubborn opposition, with a power unyielding and undecaying because it is of God. To one who listens with reverent heart, the voice of the Master still sounds amid the uproar of passionate tempests, and still commands the final calm. The entire history is, in fact, a kind of secondary rubricated Scripture, immense in extent, covering the continents, written in colossal Roman and Gothic characters, the initial letters stamped sometimes in gold and sometimes in blood, but the vast, confused and tangled text holding in it still the song of angels, the benedictions on the

Mount, the story of Bethlehem, Capernaum and the cross, the illustrious Ascension, and the terrible triumph of the Apocalypse.

A divine purpose in all history becomes gradually apparent to him who with discerning thought surveys its annals. The Bible proceeds upon the assumption of such a plan, though perhaps no one of its separated writers had a full conception of that which he was in part portraying. Back beyond the beginnings of history, onward to the secure consummation, lovely and immortal, which prophecies prefigure, extends this plan. Parts of it are yet inscrutable to us, as parts of the heavens are still unsounded by any instruments. But the conviction becomes constantly clearer, among those to whom the records of the past unfold in a measure not contents only but glowing portents, that a divine mind has presided over all; that every remotest people or tribe has had its part to do or to bear in the general progress; and that at last, when all is interpreted, the unity of the race, with the incessant interaction of its parts under the control and in the concord of a divine scheme, will come distinctly into view. Mysterious movements, as of the peoples who from woods and untamed wastes inundated Europe, and before whose irresistible momentum bastions and ramparts, the armies and ensigns of the mistress of the world went hopelessly down, will be seen to have had their impulse and direction as well as their end. Great passive empires, as of China, will be found to have served some primordial purpose; and the Mind which sees the end from the beginning will be evidenced in the ultimate human development as truly as it is in the swing of suns or in the constitution of unmeasured constellations.

The British Empire a week ago was ringing and flaming with the august and brilliant ceremonies which marked the completion of fifty years in the reign of one whose name is with us, almost as generally as in her own realms, a household word. American hearts joined those of their kinsmen across the sea, around the world, in giving God thanks for the purity and the piety with which the young maiden of fifty years since has borne herself amid gladness and grief, overshadowing change and vast prosperity, and for the progress of industry and of liberty, of commerce, education and Christian faith by which her times have been distinguished. But something more than the wisdom of statesmen, or the valor of captains, or any silent or resonant work of man, has been involved in all this. An unseen power has been guiding events to the fulfillment of plans as wide as the world, and far more ancient than Dover cliffs, with the narrow seas which gleam around them. The ultimate kingdom of righteousness and of peace is nearer for these remarkable years. It was well to render grateful praise, in church and chapel, in cathedral and abbey, in quiet homes and great universities, to Him who has given such lustre to the fame and such success to the reign of the wise and womanly and queenly Victoria.

But as with her reign, so with all that advancing history of mankind in connection with which this brilliant half century, of feminine supremacy and imperial expansion, has to be set to reveal its significance. It everywhere discloses the silent touch and the sweeping command of Divine forecasts. It reverberates with echoes to superlative designs. I know of no other department of study, outside of the Scriptures, more essentially or profoundly religious. A Christian college may well hold it in honoring esteem, and give it in permanence an eminent place among the studies which it proposes.

In our recent country, in our times of rapid and tumultuous change, it seems to me that we specially need this, as the thoughtful among us are specially inclined to it, since it is vital to the dignity and self-poise of our national life that we feel ourselves constantly interknit with the life of the world, from which the ocean does not divide us; that we recognize our magnificent inheritance in the opulent results of the effort and the struggle of other generations. It is a distinct and encouraging indication of the best qualities of the American spirit, as well as of the vigor and vivacity of the American mind and the variety of its attainments, that such studies are eagerly prosecuted among us, and that those who have given to them, with splendid enthusiasm, laborious lives—like Prescott, Motley, our honored Bancroft—have been among the most inspiring of our teachers, have gained and will keep their principal places in that Republic of letters from which the Republic of political fame must always take grace and renown.

But I have taken this study of history, Ladies and Gentlemen, not so much to particularize the various and profuse benefits of it—for which, of course, volumes would be needed, instead of paragraphs—as to indicate by it with a sharper distinctness the broadened range and brightened outlook which belong to the college course of to-day, as compared with that to which we were accustomed a half century ago. Then, as I said, nothing of history was here taught, except as perhaps obscurely suggested by Latin or Greek vocables and constructions. Now it has this prominent place among the elective studies of two years; and the change is significant of much. The same tendency appears on other sides, especially, for instance, in the courses of study now proposed in the modern languages. These, too, are both for training and for culture. They come with the study on which I have dwelt, in an association at once natural and close. The languages of Goethe and Schiller, of Dante, of Cervantes—the intelligent mastery of these is not for ornament only or chiefly, nor even for directer access to the manifold knowledges distributed in them, but that one may come to more intimate contact with the life expressed in European literature in its original forms, and that the sense of being able to converse with the masters of thought in their own tongues may add vigor to faculty, a general wealth and lustre to life. So with all the connected changes in what was of old the narrow range of the studies here offered. The aim has clearly been, as I have said, to give to those going forth from the college, to whatever departments of experience and of labor, an ampler knowledge, a finer and a nobler power, new instruments for happiness and for useful activity. The training of faculty, in studious minds, is still the governing primary aim, with the impression of the Christian truth and law and temper. But the wider culture is now recognized as auxiliary to this, while in itself of a beautiful value; and the college is unquestionably to widen its range to further bounds as years go on, and thus to make itself helpful and dear to more numerous minds, in more various departments of skillful work, as generations follow in their silent succession. So will it continue, and so will it become yet more and more, a beautiful power in the civilization to which it contributes. It is the expectation of this, and not merely the memory of the past, which animates our hearts as we gather here to-day. Not with every year, perhaps, shall this growing oak add another concentric ring of equipment or of discipline to its previous substance, but when another half century shall have passed how many shall have been these silent augmentations! How broad the shadow, and how solid the strength, of that which here in our own time was anxiously planted, in poverty, but with prayer!

Gathered as we are by this special anniversary, it is a question which naturally meets us, and toward which this rapid and imperfect discussion has constantly tended, What is the native and normal relation of a fraternity like ours to this great change in the customary courses of college instruction, and to the wider effects which it contemplates? and this is a question the answer to which is not far to seek.

By gathering to itself, as has been the effort of this fraternity, those of choice intellectual parts, and of earnest and catholic literary tastes, as well as of wholesome moral instincts and agreeable social manners, it systematically reinforces among its members the spirit of generous scholarly enterprise. Knitting students together in personal affiliation for intellectual purposes, it makes their minds interactive on each other, not in public competitions, but in the private communications of defined and limited circles, while any distinguished success of either becomes a part of the pride of the chapter. Students so related necessarily and constantly educate each other, maintaining among them the common aspiration for widened knowledge, for more various accomplishments, a more carefully trained intellectual force. The familiar criticism which they continually meet is cheering and quickening, not discouraging. In all kindness and confidence they search each other, till each is likely to learn the lesson of the legend inscribed over the statue of Tycho Brahe in the Thein church at Prague (Professor Tyler is responsible for the old-fashioned pronunciation): "*Esse potius quam haberi.*" The common desire to make the finest use of their powers, if not in one particular department then in another, is as natural to students so associated as friendship is to sympathetic households. One might almost say that it comes as certainly as any effect of physical law, in the perfumed breath which steals forth from gardens, or in the lush foliage of June. It is native, not imported; and it has a power of its own, not only to sustain the nobly ambitious, but even to curb the unruly and to animate the sluggish.

An influence of this kind is always important, not easy to secure, of great value when gained, in any college; and some plan of the sort with which we are familiar seems almost indispensable to it, since the mind of the student takes incentive and guidance from the minds of others of his own standing, or but slightly advanced, quite as readily at least, and quite as richly, as from any minds of older teachers, which are to him relatively remote. It is an influence peculiarly important, it seems to me, in our time, when the taste for athletic competition and achievement has become so wide and so engrossing. The change in this respect from the college of our earlier day, with its swings and rough bars in the open air, its creaking spring-board and wheezing foot-ball, is as striking as any that has occurred. It came almost as suddenly as a cyclone, though it came to stay. A bright young man in one of our older Eastern colleges was rusticated in his junior year for visiting a bowling alley too often. Being a man of good habits, of fair scholarship, and of excellent character, he came back to his class, was graduated with honor, and two years after was appointed tutor, one of the duties of his tutorship being to see that the men in his division went regularly to the work of the gymnasium, in which the bowling alley was a principal feature. The change is wise, and greatly beneficial. It is plainly a return, even if in the somewhat boisterous American fashion, toward the Greek idea of simultaneous and harmonious training of body and of mind as necessary to a complete education. But there has been some danger, perhaps, that the element coming in with this later vehemence might disturb and obscure that to which it has been added, as the rushing Arve muddies the clear blue of the Rhone into which it is absorbed. The temper of intellectual aspiration, quickened and sustained by frequent and intimate intellectual fellowships, must keep its pre-eminence, or the college would soon become a mere shouting and stormy athletic club. A fraternity like ours, working normally, works always in the needed direction. It animates the taste for variety in study, and is thus in constitutional sympathy with the entire intellectual movement within the colleges in recent years. It puts the stimulated minds of its members face to face, for mutual discipline, reciprocal incentive; and it is always study which it helps, a manifold culture, rather than any development of muscle. Its running matches are in the fields of the Muses. Its applauded achievements are in the domain of letters and the arts. The leap and wrestle which it encourages, are between minds moving from thought to thought, and from author to author.

It has even a distinctly moral influence, as evident as the mental, and yet more beneficent. Instances are within my knowledge in which certain bright and eager young men, peculiarly susceptible to college temptations, while peculiarly fit for college successes, have been restrained from bad associations, have been excited to better ambitions, have been enveloped, to their permanent advantage, in a governing spirit within the chapter which wrought for a gentler and nobler manhood. I cannot but think that a wise faculty will always shelter, favor and cherish any association which works in this temper for ends so important.

A beneficial influence belongs also, inherently, to such an organized fraternity, arising from the fact that whatever has been done by its older members, after graduation, in the way of distinguished literary work, of eloquent speech, of effective assistance to generous movements, is kept more distinctly before the minds of those tarrying in the chapters from whose active exercises the others have withdrawn. A certain sense of special fellowship unites therein the younger with the older, which in its way, and in the measure of its reach, is an educating power. The students of a college are always glad, and properly proud, when one of its graduates attains high distinction in the literary, the professional, or the political field. But the members of a chapter have a clearer and a closer sense of just gratification when one whose name is borne on their rolls achieves a useful and high distinction. Old stories are recalled of his earlier efforts; his subsequent methods, in study and in the culture of style, are more carefully scanned; a fresh ambition is started in those who have their own place to attain in the world; and I cannot doubt that many responsive and on-looking minds, in this chapter and in others, have been inspired to greater ardor in appropriate studies, and greater persistency in intellectual exercise, to acquire for themselves a noble and an exquisite English style, to master the power of high and rich and discriminated thought, to prepare themselves for large offices in the world—because belonging to chapters bearing in eminence on their rolls names like those of Frederic Huntington, Algernon Sullivan, Truman Backus, of the Choate who adds new honor to the name, of the Curtis whose touch of velvet smoothness, in daintiest sentences, hides behind it a sensitive conscience, with purposes strong as sinews of steel. Each member feels a fresh responsibility resting upon him to keep himself worthy of companionship like theirs; to prepare himself to stand, when the time has come, in the ranks upon which abides a lustre from names so honored. Even names which death has crowned with stars — like that of the accomplished scholar, the eloquent teacher, the wide-minded theologian, whose presence we had gladly expected to-day, and sadly miss — have a continuing power to bless. They do not fade from eye or thought, but beckon us up to higher levels, while we a little longer linger.

A peculiar sense of union with others closely and happily associated with one in such a fraternity goes forward with him, too, into subsequent life, wherever and in whatsoever vocation his lot may be cast; and this brings its own beauty and blessing. It is inevitable, as I have said, that the outcome of the college system, as it now is presented, should be shown on more diversified fields of subsequent labor than were contemplated a half century ago. Not all men trained in such institutions as this is rapidly coming to be are to be ministers, lawyers, or physicians. Some will be architects, painters, sculptors; some will be editors, authors, teachers; some will be scientists, inventors, explorers, or civil engineers; and some will be cultured merchants, perhaps, manufacturers, bankers, railway officers, or men of property and leisure. Their paths will diverge more and more, as life goes on, and their separated employments will tend to keep them apart from each other. Without some influence in the opposite direction, the effect may be to prevent the invigorating contact of their minds with each other, by absorbing each, with a narrowing rigor, in his special pursuit. It is well and salutary, under circumstances like these, that there be strong and vital sympathies uniting them in after life, arising from common glad recollections of sympathetic association in the earlier days; that they go back together to the pleasant reunions, intellectual and social, of the chapter-house and its meetings; that the earlier collisions and happy affiliations of mind with mind come freshly to their remembering thought. So will be likely to be kept alive in them a certain healthful and beautiful correspondence of spirit and aim, in the broader life into which they have entered. The college itself will have for their memories a livelier charm. The earlier aspiration will more surely survive in their souls. Unconsciously, even, they will heed and fulfill the noble advice which the Marquis de Posa, according to Schiller, sent by the Queen to his pupil, Don Carlos: "To revere in manhood the dreams of his youth, and not to be led astray when by the wisdom of the dust he hears enthusiasm blasphemed." In our hurried American society, full as it is of secular ambitions, of rapidity, noise, and the clamor for success in whatever department, this seems to me peculiarly needful; and certainly the impulse of a fraternity like this, and like others established with similarly discreet plans and aims, must supply here a force of essential value, and of permanent efficiency.

It tends as well, I am equally sure, in the measure of its influence, to remove the prejudices which used to exist between the students of different colleges, and even to bring the institutions themselves into happier relations, as members of the several chapters of the fraternity, in the various colleges, meet in a co-operative sympathy, and honor and rejoice in each other's success. The old temper was one, we must admit, rather of distrust, or of positive dislike, between the colleges of the sea-board and these among the hills; between the latter, among themselves. In my time here, the typical Harvard student was to us one who did not greatly exercise his brain, but who wore glasses, carried a cane, was curled and perfumed, and studiously parted his hair in the middle. His conception of us was, doubtless, a caricature equally grotesque, but in a widely different direction. From those of not a few other colleges we expected vigor, pluck, intellectual push, but with palpable deficiencies in refinement and grace. Many causes have modified this spirit of mutual disrespect, largely ameliorating if they have not abolished it. One of the causes operating in this way, with an excellent effect, has been the frequent communications between the chapters of general fraternities extending into many colleges. The more distinguished students in each have become known to the others. The governing sense of common aims, and a common work, has been constantly reinforced in each toward the rest. A certain solidarity, of harmonious aspiration and of reciprocal interest, comes by degrees to be established among them. The time is certainly hastened in its approach when all the colleges scattered over the land will recognize themselves as only local constituent members of the real and great American University; which will have no single cathedral city, but the campus of the continent, for its seat, and which will be richer than in any renown derived from the past through the fame which it wins by training men for great utilities, noble offices. By training *men*, I have said; but the training of women, through similar methods, with an equal effect, is a part of the modern widened movement among American colleges, as important as the other which I have sketched, in close harmony with it, and assuming rapidly equal proportions. Newnham and Girton have lately surprised the English universities by the accurate and large learning imparted in them. Smith College and Amherst will have as well their friendly rivalries and eager competitions, and the vexed problem of co-education may be held, I think, by the most exacting and fastidious critic, to have found in them its proper solution, unless Amherst and Northampton are farther from each other than they used to be when I was young. The final University which is thus magnificently arising among us will embrace in itself all such equipped and advancing schools, of training and culture, in any State, for either sex. Its vastness and opulence will have had no parallel among the comparatively restricted institutions across the sea, to which kings and prelates have made contribution. Its spires will shine from the sounding Atlantic onward to the ocean of Peace. Multitudinous associations, clinging more tenaciously than tentacles of ivy, will robe its far extending walls, as the pavements of its corridors are worn by the feet of successive generations. Its chiming bells, with musical triumph, will ring in the era of assured liberty, of popular intelligence with a refined and ripened culture, of thriving enterprise, and of Christian faith.

So, Mr. President, ladies and gentlemen, and brothers of the fraternity, I join with you in gladness at the fact that the fifty years since this chapter was organized have seen it growing in strength and fame, keeping at least in equal advance with the college in which it is embosomed; and I join with you equally in the hope that when another half century shall have passed it may have only an ampler power, a richer promise, a nobler fame. The traveler in Switzerland not unfrequently sees in the eastern sky what he takes to be a patch of cloud, fair but fleeting, white beneath the morning light, silently transfigured, as if charged from within by golden, chrysolite, opaline lustres, when the sun has passed the meridian. Its permanence gives it interpretation. It is not a cloud, but a mountain peak, solid as the earth from which it arises, though delicate in outline, and burning in the air like a translucent gem. This chapter which we love seemed to some, no doubt, in the days when the morning light lay on our path, a passing whirl of mist-laden air, hovering for a season in the sky of the college. It has kept its place, never expanding to large proportions, but growing more eminent and more variously lucent before our thought as the sun for us has descended in the west.

I trust that it will be as permanent as the college, and will be constantly clothed upon with a more attractive and various charm, as the sun which is to mark the following centuries in the life of the college seeks its, as yet, unseen horizon.

BANQUET

REMARKS OF THE TOAST-MASTER

HON. JOHN E. SANFORD, '51.

Brothers of the Alpha Delta Phi, Ladies and Gentlemen:

If the man who invented the calendar had had the advantage of fifty years' experience in this society, and had thereby gained some adequate conception of what would be a suitable allotment of time for a semi-centennial celebration, I do him the justice to believe that he would have made his day consist of more than twenty-four hours; but, as a consequence of his original and irrevocable blunder, the few and fleeting hours that remain to us, as well as this list which I hold in my hand, remind us that the last and best course of the evening, the course of speech and song, must not be long delayed.

We close to-night, brethren, with this banquet, a glad and memorable day in the history of our beloved Amherst Chapter, a day most auspiciously and splendidly opened in the public exercises of the morning, a day to be closed, I hope, not less fittingly and happily here to-night. I trust I know too well the nature of the duty which has been assigned to me to abuse its privilege or to trespass upon your indulgence. He who has the honor to preside — they sometimes call him the speaker of the assembly — must never be its speech-maker. I am here as a means to an end simply, and you, not I, constitute that end. I know that there is no brother here whose heart is not full of thoughts if not of words. I may not speak here of the memories and traditions of these fifty years, the influences, the aspirations, the helpful and uplifting fellowships which Alpha Delta Phi has given to us; in a word, all that our beloved fraternity has done for us and been to us. I am only too glad that these will find more fitting expressions at your lips. Let me content myself, then, with voicing only the congratulations of the day and the hour. Let me speak the welcome of every brother here to every other brother, to all honored guests as well, and let me not forget these spectators, these better angels of our nature, whose presence here to-night adds a new and welcome charm and zest to this occasion.

Fifty years is surely long enough to test the relation of our Society, and of like societies, and the occasion naturally suggests what the true relation has been and shall be. No one can more fully discuss that question than the president of the college. I have, therefore, the honor to propose the first subject, "The Relation of Greek Letter Societies to College Discipline," and to introduce to you President Seelye.

THE RELATIONS OF GREEK LETTER SOCIETIES TO COLLEGE DISCIPLINE.

PRESIDENT JULIUS H. SEELYE.

Every one familiar with the facts in the case must judge favorably of the Greek letter societies in Amherst College. Without a doubt they exercise a wholesome energy both upon their individual members and upon the college. Combination is strength, whether with young men or old, and where men combine for good ends better results may, of course, be looked for than where the same ends are sought by individuals alone.

Now the aim of these societies is certainly good. They are not formed for pleasure simply, though they are one of the most fruitful sources of pleasure in a student's college life. Their first aim is the improvement of their members — improvement in literary culture and in manly character. They are all of them literary societies. An effort was made not long since to introduce among us a new society with prominently social rather than literary aims, but it not only failed to receive the requisite assent of the president of the college, but was not favored by any considerable number of the students, many of whom stoutly opposed it.

The aim of these societies is, I say, improvement in literary culture and in manly character, and this aim is reasonably justified by the results. It is not accidental that the foremost men in college, as a rule, belong to some of these societies. That each society should seek for its membership the best scholars, the best writers and speakers, the best men of a class, shows well where its strength is thought to lie. A student entering one of these societies finds a healthy stimulus in the repute which his fraternity shall share from his successful work. The rivalry of individuals loses much of its narrowness, and almost all of its envy, when the prize which the individual seeks is valued chiefly for its benefit to the fellowship to which he belongs. Doubtless members of these societies often remain narrow-minded and laggard in the race, after all the influence of their society has been expended upon them, but the influence is a broadening and a quickening one, notwithstanding. Under its power the self-conceit of a young man is more likely to give way to self-control than otherwise.

One of the happiest features of society life at Amherst, introduced, like every other, by your own society, fair mother of us all, is the life in the chapter-houses. There are no better residences, and none better kept, in the village than these. They are not extravagant, but they are neat and tasteful; they have pleasant grounds surrounding them, the cost of rooms in them is not greater than the average cost in other houses, and they not only furnish the students occupying them a pleasant home, but the care of the home and its surroundings is itself a culture.

There need be no objection to these societies on account of their secrecy. The secrecy is largely in name; is, in fact, little more than the privacy proper to the most familiar intercourse of families and friends. Treated as the societies are among us, and occupying the ground they do, no mischief comes from their secrecy. Instead of promoting cliques and cabals, in point of fact we find less of them than the history of the college shows before the societies came. The rivalry between them is a healthy one, and is conducted openly and in a manly way.

The societies must give back to the college the tone they have first received. I observe that good Dr. McCosh, at Princeton, is solicitous about their influence there, but I am persuaded that in any college where the prevailing life is true and earnest, the societies fed by its fountain will send back bright and quickening streams. They certainly give gladness and refreshment to our whole college life at Amherst.

If, for me, having my name enrolled in a society not yet crowned with the laurels of fifty years of such a history as is represented here to-night, it be proper to make a suggestion to the Amherst chapter of the Alpha Delta Phi, I beg leave to ask whether, leading all our history, as you have so honorably done, you may not introduce another new departure, in the endowment of fraternity scholarships or fellowships for advanced students, undergraduate or graduate? Better, I think, than any other large expenditure in behalf of the society, would such endowments serve both the society and the college.

I thank you, Mr. President and gentlemen, for the honor done me, and the pleasure afforded by the invitation to be present at these festivities. I accept the invitation, as officially given to the president of the college, and I gratefully recognize, in behalf of the college, both what this fraternity has already done in making its history so brilliant with illustrious names, and what it is doing to-day in adorning and strengthening the college in making its members purer, braver, truer men, and in using its increasing power for increasing growth in all that is honorable and of good report. I look upon its past and its present as the bright dawn of a brighter day.

A HALF CENTURY AGO.

REV. E. E. BLISS, D.D., '37.

Brothers of the Alpha Delta Phi:

I need not assure you that it gives me great pleasure to be present at this our semi-centennial. So far as I remember, it is the first time I have met anything like the general gathering of the Fraternity during the fifty years that have elapsed since I was graduated. You must, therefore, my brethren, understand with what an appetite, after fifty years of famishing, I come to your banquet to-night. And now, in rising to speak a few words — for they will be few — in regard to those fifty years ago, I beg your indulgence for the imperfections of my speech.

I have been, as has been stated, fifty years in a foreign land on the other side of the Atlantic, and have been obliged to speak to my fellowmen in another language than the English, so that my English tongue is a good deal tied. And what is worse, living among a people whose great watchword is, "Slowly, slowly," the impress has come upon my body and my mind. The conductors of your street-cars say to me, "Step lively!" Well, we do not step lively in Turkey. I feel sometimes a great danger of being overrun and trodden under foot, and I am inclined to turn to those behind me and say, "Slowly, slowly." If I were seeking employment in this country I do not know but I would ask for a position as street preacher, and take my position upon some street in Boston and say to the crowd, "Slowly, slowly." The effect has been to make me and my mind move slowly, in sympathy with those men of the slow country, and you may well understand that I feel rather dazed here to-night amidst the evidence of the movements of these modern times. I feel like a man who has come out from a mine. In fact, my principal work in the mission with which I am connected, has been in the publication work, and, like the miners, we walk and work under great disadvantages; but, by and by, though I am not a prophet or the son of a prophet, you will see some great changes in the Turkish country.

But I must hasten to the fifty years ago, or I shall never get there. I suppose the colleges of fifty years ago were rather slow. When I came to college I was not helped by steam; I footed it. And we did not have very much assistance from the lightning in communicating our ideas. We dug into the ground, and we were not very sure of what we found there. It was a slow time; but, brethren of the Alpha Delta Phi, progress was beginning to come. Mr. Eells's spirit was beginning to be felt. The result was the organization of the Amherst Chapter of the Alpha Delta Phi.

There were some preliminary movements in the direction of historical study, of which Dr. Storrs has spoken so eloquently to-day. This branch grew out of the desire for the pursuance of these historical studies. We did organize, there was nobody to refuse us, and so we gathered on the principle of elective affinity, and we soon found that we were in communication with congenial spirits of other institutions. We were a small company and our numbers were modest as compared with what greets my eye on this semi-centennial. I remember very distinctly the small room in the small entry to what was then called South College. I speak not derogatively of college studies nor those who were our teachers, but we felt that it would be a benefit for us to extend our thoughts and widen the scope of our imagination and seek for things which were excellent in other lines than those which were in the regular college course of studies. We adopted the motto — I think it was Coleridge's: " Plain living and high thinking." We thought that motto might be transferred to another field, and we made it ours. Well, we have gone on in the line of plain living — some of us have been obliged to — but whether we have accomplished anything in the way of high thinking I will not undertake to say. Some of our Fraternity have attained to their ideals to some extent. Others have not, but we rejoice in the benefit and happiness we have derived from association. I have often met with members of this society who have come traveling in the East, and it has always been a great pleasure to give them the hand of fellowship.

I rejoice in the evidence of growth which I see continually, and in the success which has attended this organization. It has come to be a power far greater than anything we could have expected in those days. May your future be as prosperous as has been your past, and success always attend this, our society.

THE CHIVALRY OF ALPHA DELTA PHI.

HON. ALGERNON S. SULLIVAN, *Miami*, '45.

Mr. President and Gentlemen:

After the splendor of oratory which has shone upon us to-day, I can almost imagine that the real purpose of the Amherst Chapter on this occasion was not to celebrate its fiftieth anniversary, but to exhibit to the world that, although its matchless trinity of orators has been broken by the translation of Henry Ward Beecher and Roswell D. Hitchcock, it still remains true that the brightest star and the fairest flower in the field of American eloquence still abides in the possession of the Amherst Chapter. Dr. Storrs gave the key to all the thought that must continue to the end of the celebration and the festivities, placed upon it by the inexorable law, his own conception of what it is to be an Alpha Delta Phi.

My toast, as I look at it, seems to me to be a little too heroic, and yet the very circumstances which the speaker mentioned—

my knowledge of the foundation, although not contemporary with it, of the first child of Alpha Delta Phi in the organization of the Hamilton Chapter and my acquaintance with the brothers whose names have been mentioned—make it necessary that I should at once accept the term " The Chivalry of the Alpha Delta Phi," in a sense that was made obvious to-day. Taking it to mean that faith which knights to knighthood bore, how at once our hearts come in sympathy with it as a proper toast somewhere in the order of proceedings this evening! Faith, inspiration, aspiration, duty, high endeavor and high achievement, if, indeed, it be the right thing to say in the presence of an intelligent company like this that there is not high achievement except with high endeavor. Certainly it is not true that there is high achievement without high endeavor when we are considering the subject on the plane of action which ought to be above all.

Tracing the succession of thought that occurred to me on the acceptance I give to the term "chivalry," it occurred to me when thinking a few moments ago of the approach of the summons to respond to this toast, what a kinship there is, what a potent action there is in all ideal plans. The ideal of knighthood I have sketched, but how true it is that all ideal paths move nearly in parallel lines in this respect of the advance of thought along a line that is not only forward but is always upward, until it will bring us to just that plane which I have defined.

Now, gentlemen, it is true that I come as a delegate from one of the western chapters of this Fraternity, and come under circumstances and with reminiscences that make it peculiarly interesting to me if, for a moment, I can hope to make it interesting to you. You will bear in mind—and I indulge in the reference to it the more readily because it has not yet been referred to— that our society, that its character and its qualities, had the personal characteristics that belonged to our founder, Samuel Eells. He wrote no creed; there is no constitution which was to be subscribed to. There were no pledges. No man can find any writing from him, or contemporary with him, giving that law which every member of the Fraternity realizes and feels to be impressed upon him, and yet he knows that it is absolutely true that Samuel Eells's character, Samuel Eells's methods, Samuel Eells's aims, his intentions, his purposes, his efforts, his whole being, gave at once, when he formed this society and when he formed the chapter in which I had the honor to be initiated—he gave to it and to its members the impress of his own character, of his own feelings. It has abided until to-day, it has culminated in an assembly here in these classic grounds, a convention representative of all that is strong, active, noble, elevating, influential, beautiful in the life that is coming out as being the expression of American thought and American ideas and American purposes.

I remember when I left my little village home in Indiana and moved to Oxford, Ohio, to attend the Miami University. Immediately on my arrival the subject of discussion, as usual when any new class arrived, was with regard to the societies connected with the college. First and foremost was always mentioned the name of the little society Alpha Delta Phi. Mr. Eells had then died, but the coterie personally selected by him still continued in existence, and I soon learned, when I had the honor of being requested to become a member of the society, that the entire membership looked to Samuel Eells with a sentiment that was akin to devotion. He seemed to make such an impression, not only upon members of the society but upon the college, that there was no more honored name than that of Samuel Eells. And I may be permitted here to say that in that college, which could fairly be described as being almost a frontier college, there was gathered a body of the members of the Alpha Delta Phi, who, with one exception, the speaker, have gone out into life and have continued to live shining lives, and who do so at this very hour. I only wish some of this company whom I could name on that list, instead of myself, as the representatives and delegates from that firstborn chapter of Alpha Delta Phi, were here to speak for it and duly represent it. I remember when, after leaving college to study law, selecting Cincinnati for my home, I entered there again into active fraternal intercourse with the men who had learned to know Mr. Eells during the four years that remained to him of his life after he went to Cincinnati for the purpose of making it his home.

I may be permitted to recall again what is mentioned in our book of authority and records, that, as Brother Salmon P. Chase loved to say privately and at all times, Samuel Eells displayed, as the founder of Alpha Delta Phi, his character as a Christian. I have heard Governor Chase, again and again, speak in terms of almost idolizing fondness of his youthful partner, who died so soon after the opening of his career in Cincinnati.

Now, gentlemen, this matter of the chivalry of a society means, necessarily, a great deal when there is a convention at the end of fifty years of the existence of any chapter or of any order ; in this, that the history of the society has already made itself —in its past and for the future as well. This society is to-day and will be just that which it has lived up to and lived out in its fifty years, and I ask you if it be not fairly true that there has been a vital force impressed upon it. In its nearly twenty chapters there has come to be a uniformity in the high standard, as Samuel Eells intended it, of morals, of character, as being preferable to mere intellectual culture or the accumulation of knowledge. He himself has said that this end of character of the development of the entire man in its manhood, moral, social, as well as intellectual, was the purpose and aim that he had in assembling kindred spirits and in founding this organization. Has it not come to be true of the organization? I ask you to turn your thoughts back for a brief ten hours from the moment when I am speaking and ask you if it were otherwise than I have supposed — if it could have been possible that Dr. Storrs, in coming to make this semi-centennial oration, could have felt that the occasion, the audience, the Fraternity about him, was of itself the occasion and the impulse of that masterly and beautiful review and study, the educative effect of history in an academic course and in the course of formation of character—character that was to be in sympathy, wholly, with the law and the example which he put forward almost unintentionally and irresistibly as the sum of human character as developed in realization of the law of Him who spake as man never spake. It came from him as the expression of his own conception that that which he knew would alone meet the requirement and expectation of a convention of the sons of Alpha Delta Phi. It constitutes, in my mind, the best of all testimonials as to the history and the nature and the essential quality of the association.

Now, gentlemen, it is very easy for us to say this in general, but there is not a day nor an hour in which there is not, in the call directly presented to every such association and to every individual of it, a call for the manifestation of the sentiments and principles which constitute the foundation and keystone of our order. I never thought of it more than I did in an incident which occurred to me during the day. I stood, on a stormy and dark night only a week or two ago, on the heights above Hoboken. It happened that I was down there and was detained by a storm, and as the storm had passed I went to the brink of the hill and there had that exciting and beautiful view, the like of which is to be found in few countries, for it is not often that there is a great city near which there is a high beetling cliff as a point of outlook. As I stood there watching the lights that mark the homes and movements of nearly three million people, extending almost from my feet eastward and southward for nearly a score of miles, not a man was discernible, not a sound from their existence was heard, and yet I could feel that I was on the shore of this sea of humanity—all moved by the same hopes and the same plans. And following some of these moving lights my eye was arrested by one which fixed and attracted and held my attention, and in a moment my fancy reminded me of what it was. I could not see what was beneath it, but I knew that, raised and pointing far into the upper air, it was the blazing beacon upheld by the hand of the Statue of Liberty. There it was! And so it is that over every community there is, to the eye that will look for it, some beacon and some signal that will be a pointer and a monitor to tell that it was there for a purpose, that it relates to and calls out the proper sentiments and the sense of duty towards one's fellow-man. I knew I could not see that figure, but I knew it was there. I knew what that beacon told. I knew that it reminded me of the fraternity between fraternal nations. I knew that it reminded me of the guardianship and great trusts that were put upon the people of the city of New York. I knew that it reminded me of the hearty sympathies of all the world towards America. I could but then, as I do now, feel almost an unuttered prayer : Oh, ye gods of the winds, touch lightly that central herald in our harbor! Oh, ye mists that come in from the ocean, string and gem it so that it will shine like diamonds in the morning sun, but never hide it from the faithful sons of Alpha Delta Phi, who gather in such an increasing colony in the cities about that harbor! Let it be for ages that it, too, shall stand there as a consecration of the chivalrous sentiments, the freedom and the spirit of evangelism and good citizenship, to all that are within its reach. So it will be, and so it is, and so I can speak not only for the western representation of the Alpha Delta Phi, but for the Fraternity entire. To the voice of chivalry calling from that statue they respond by recognizing the duties, the claims of manhood and good citizenship.

So it will ever be, my brothers. I never realized it so fully as now, when I see the magnetic attraction that has assembled this rare convention, and I am only glad that it is recognized, that it is more than a mere mechanical line of beauty for the sons of Alpha Delta Phi, and that there is that spirit of gallantry and courage of truth, of high endeavor, to which, without great extravagance, the term "chivalry" can be applied.

ALPHA DELTA PHI IN THE PULPIT.

E. K. ALDEN, D.D., '44.

[*Only Partially Reported.*]

Mr. President and Brethren:

Of the original five members who commenced Alpha Delta Phi, three were lawyers, one was a teacher, and one was a minister. That proportion has been continued to the present day. Of the 4,500 members now constituting our honored Fraternity, a little over 800 represent the pulpit, and of these about 125 the Amherst Chapter. Of these 800, speaking now in round numbers, about 225 are Congregationalists, 175 are Presbyterians, 140 are Episcopalians, bishops included, 80 Methodists, 80 Baptists, and about 100 are distributed among the other varied and various denominations.

I am called to speak of "Alpha Delta Phi in the Pulpit," describing them all in one ideal man. The Congregationalist and Presbyterian, which mix up pretty well together, is a fine looking face always. You take the general run of ministers as you will see them gathered together in a large room, and the solid, substantial element will be the Congregational and Presbyterian. The Episcopalian comes in for ornament — a very handsome ornament, too — and the Baptists and Methodists for vigorous action. Now, in describing this ideal man, the "Alpha Delta Phi in the Pulpit," the first distinguishing characteristic — for no other fraternity can say we do not lead in one remarkable particular — is that he is *Apostolic*. When this topic was sent me a few days ago with the request for a brief address, I immediately took down my Greek concordance and ran over the allusions to Alpha Delta Phi in the New Testament, and I found precisely 424 distinct references, with the names of quite a number of the brothers. The very first disciple who was called by our Lord to lead the glorious company of His disciples to the end of time is definitely described in the first chapter of the fourth gospel, as Alpha Delta Phi ["$\dot{\alpha}\delta\varepsilon\lambda\varphi$"] Simon Peter. Consult your Greek Testament and you will find it there. The man who first led Simon into the presence of the Master, was also an "Ἀδελφ" named Andrew. The two sons of Zebedee, John and James, are both definitely called "Ἀδελφ." Look up the old Greek Testament—good reading occasionally for lawyers and teachers as well as ministers—and you will find abundant illustrations. One case is quite remarkable. When Saul of Tarsus saw a light from heaven and was arrested on his persecuting career at Damascus, and when he needed one word instantly to arouse, cheer and start him on his upward path, "a man named Ananias" was the elect instrument to speak that word, and this was the word: " Ἀδελφ, Saul, arise." He arose, and you know what came of it, and how superbly he led forward the great movement of the Lord's advancing kingdom. Read his epistles and you will find frequent allusions to Alpha Delta Phi, "Ἀδελφ Timothy;" "Ἀδελφ, Titus;" "Ἀδελφ, Epaphroditus;" "Love the ἀδελφ," and so on to the end of the chapter. That was the first "*Chapter*" of Alpha Delta Phi. We may in the presence of the representatives of all other Greek letter societies rightfully claim that ΑΔΦ has an apostolic beginning.

The second characteristic of this ideal man is that he is *scholarly*. [Here the speaker introduced a long and honored list of representatives of the fraternity, including Profs. Austin Phelps, Henry B. Smith, Roswell D. Hitchcock, and many more, closing, as last and by no means least, with "the man who sits before me, Prof. E. P. Crowell."] So much for the scholarly feature in the ideal "Alpha Delta Phi in the Pulpit."

Add to this the general style of man for practical service, solid, substantial, sound, faithful and true—the average *A Δ Φ* wherever found, at home or abroad—*a splendid worker*. [Here followed the names of several representative men, some of them missionaries in the broadest aggressive work of the Church in foreign lands, including the veteran who was present, a graduate of fifty years ago, Dr. Edwin E. Bliss, of Constantinople, including also several in the audience in the immediate vicinity of the speaker, special reference being made to the brothers in the classes of '42 to '46, Lawyer Stockbridge and Professor March, who sat one on each side of the speaker, being on account of their rare excellences, claimed as in a sense preachers—March having, in reality, begun in this line even in his Freshman year, when he first joined Alpha Delta Phi.]

Put all these men together, letting them pass one by one before the photographic plate, something of each going into the one face thus caught, and you begin to see what is meant by " Alpha Delta Phi in the Pulpit."

This will be more vividly presented by looking at the members of one class specially honored in the public services of the day. The first time I attained to the dignity of being present at an Amherst College commencement — indeed, of any college commencement — was when I was quite a boy. It was in the year 1839. I had never before seen a college class, and that class of '39 was a great and wonderful sight to my juvenile eyes. I recall the orations of that red-letter day. There was one exceedingly youthful graduate, not quite eighteen years of age. His venerable father, whom I had often seen at my father's house, was present, wearing quite an anxious look. When that young man rose to speak, the old gentleman — I remember the exact expression of his countenance as I sat watching him—was evidently somewhat apprehensive as to the success of the inexperienced youth, especially as he had chosen for his topic of discourse "The Joys of the Scholar," a subject which at that time, of course, he knew a great deal about. When he began, his father's head dropped instantaneously; but after two or three sentences had been pronounced in a clear, ringing voice, that bowed head began slowly to lift, and after the fourth or fifth sentence the whole body straightened up, and from that time that gratified father, out of his deep-set eyes, looked steadily and just a little proudly at the young orator, who swept everything before him. That was the first time I ever listened to a public address from Richard Salter Storrs, Jr. I recall also the valedictory from a young man of decided promise bearing the name of Frederic Dan Huntington. Also an oration—philosophical I think it was—from a curly-headed youth called Edward Bates Gillett. As this last-named brilliant brother is reported in the papers as occasionally occupying the sacred desk in Amherst College Church and other favored localities, I here and now, in the name of Alpha Delta Phi, claim Gillett as one of the representatives of the pulpit. Now, put together these three men as they are to-day, members of one class, adding, if you please, from the same class, another of our fraternity, "Father" Augustine Francis Hewitt, of the Holy Catholic Church. Mix them up in good proportions, give them full liberty, each and all—that freedom of utterance of which we hear so much in these times—let them have a fair chance to show what in their best condition they can do, and you have a favorable representative of "Alpha Delta Phi in the Pulpit." If this does not fully meet our ideal, we can throw in also from the same fraternity Henry Ward Beecher, Phillips Brooks and Edward Everett Hale—if Bishop Huntington will keep an eye on Dr. Hale's theology—and we shall certainly have a somewhat brilliant and effective man. I commend him to the younger members of the brotherhood as the ideal Alpha Delta Phi of the pulpit of the future.

Should I select for this coming man a double motto toward which we might begin to aspire, even now, "each according to his several ability," it would be the two epitaphs upon the memorial stones of the two brothers, Henry and John Lawrence, who achieved so noble a work in critical times in India. One represents the modest estimate a faithful and true man is permitted to have of himself. The other represents the estimate which his friends, who know his genuine worth, may give as their testimony when his work is done. Henry Lawrence was buried, where as a brave soldier he fell, at Lucknow, and his epitaph, suggested by himself, reads: "*Here lies Henry Lawrence, who tried to do his duty.*" His brother is buried in Westminster Abbey, and above his dust is inscribed the epitaph suggested by his friends—may God enable us all so to finish our course that we may merit the same!—"*Here lies John Lawrence, who did his duty to the last.*"

ALPHA DELTA PHI IN POLITICS.

HON. GEO. WILLIAM CURTIS, *Brunonian*, '54.

Mr. President and Brethren:

I was delighted to learn early in the spring that the flag of victorious Alpha Delta Phi had been raised at last over the haughty and heroic heights of Boston under the leadership of Major-General Choate. I was extremely sorry that I was unable to take part in the final assault, for I was holding the post on Staten Island, and I am glad to report to you that of the 40,000 inhabitants of Staten Island I think there are not more than 39,999 still outside of our mystic order. General Choate, following the example of his distinguished predecessor, General Washington, has transferred his headquarters from Boston to New York, which he occupies in great force, sallying forth from time to time and doing prodigies of eloquence against the Sigma Phis, Psi U's, Tau Gammas, and other hostile Greek tribes; while across the river, in Brooklyn, our brother, the orator of the day, as you may well believe, offers persuasive benefits of clergy which melt the hearts of the most depraved and awaken even the hope of regeneration in the most desperate and abandoned Delta Kappa Epsilons.

This has been an uncommonly favorable season for the Greek letter societies. It began with the New York dinner for the Greek school at Athens. It was continued by the triumphant assault at Boston. It goes on to-day when the Alpha at Dartmouth celebrates the centennial of Phi Beta Kappa. But the culmination of the season is here, and now I speak reverently of Phi Beta Kappa, as of our common mother; but Alpha Delta Phi is the prince royal of the majestic Greek line, and her semi-centennial here at Amherst is the apex of this memorable year. I am only surprised, Mr. President, that I find myself speaking in any other language than that of Demosthenes or Pindar. I observe, as I know you did, gentlemen, that our distinguished chairman of the evening could with difficulty save himself from lapsing into the Dorian mood, and wholly in vain he struggled to escape from the Eolian melody. As for what I may have to say I can only hope that what it may lack in Greek it may make up in intelligence, and I even trust that by some of the younger members of the Fraternity, at least, I may be understood if I venture to speak only in my native Yankee dialect.

The felicity of this day is of many kinds, but all great transactions require a fitting scene. I look out upon this historic landscape, these beautiful hills to the east where Shay's rebellion staggered and fell dead, that luxuriant meadow to the north where the flower of Essex was plucked by savage hands, the broad valley to the west where the river gods of the Connecticut dwelt, and I behold the proper theatre of this day's event. Here, also, is the scene of the most romantic and inspiring of New England legends, and if your neighbor, Mr. George Sheldon, of Deerfield, may dissolve the tale in the alembic of truth, he cannot destroy the significance of that tradition which romance and poetry and the instinct of heroism in the human heart will not let die. As I look out and see this garden of New England, Holyoke and Tom guarding, like sentinels, the southern gate, and Toby, in solitary state watching the northern approach, I know that I look not only upon a scene of beauty, but upon homes of prosperity, of peace, of freedom; homes of intelligence, industry and moral constancy, such as no human eye ever saw in any other land at any other time.

Alpha Delta Phi in politics! What is it, gentlemen, but the integrity, the independence, the courage, the flower of Puritan virtues which have given this region its renown and made it so fair? There is a great deal of fun made of the scholar in politics. Let the scholar in politic restort that he also serves who illuminates his own thought and experience by which we all move with the thought and experience of all the ages; that the man who trains himself by the best knowledge, who masters history not only in the spirit and in the sense, but for the purpose and the result that were so magnificently unfolded to us this morning, is a man quite as useful in American politics as the man who reads only a party organ and holds that "soap" is the true political solvent, and that honor and honesty are a super-celestial ambrosia altogether too fine and good for the daily food of politics. You will hear, gentlemen, those of you who to-day set forth upon your journey in life—you will hear a great deal of Sunday-school statesmanship. But you will see a great deal more of saloon statesmanship, and I beg you to remember that the country into which you are born and which you are to serve, came from the Sunday-school and not from the saloon. If to keep your hands clean in politics is to be a dude, then "dude" is a taunt to be borne as a wreath like the taunt of "Methodists" hurled at Wesley, or of "whig" at the old opponents of despotism, or of "Yankee doodle" at our fathers of the Revolution; and if some of these young hearts shrink and quiver at those dreadful taunts of "Pharisee" and "goody-goody"—not yet, not yet, brethren, have they the lofty faith and the fiery heart of righteousness, of which the mystic symbol is Alpha Delta Phi.

Now, there seem to be two ways in which this Fraternity can serve American politics. The first is as a body of educated, intelligent, self-respecting men, in assuaging the fury of party spirit, a spirit which becomes more furious just in the degree that the real significance of parties disappears. In this country, gentlemen, we all work through political parties, but a party is, after all, the servant and the voter is the master. But the servant constantly strives to become the master, and generally succeeds. I do not need to rehearse to you the purely partisan spirit. In one of his letters Swift says: " Even the ladies are splitting asunder into high church and low church, and such is their zeal for religion that they have hardly time to say their prayers." Addison, with the same delicate touch of humor, describes that charming old Tory fox-hunter in the time of George the First, who swore that there had been "no decent weather in England since William the Third sat upon the throne;" and that other delightful innkeeper, who said that really during the year he had not been able to go to church, but he trusted that he had served the Lord by heading the mob to pull down a few dissenting meeting-houses. This is the mildest statement of the ferocity of party spirit. The better one is Dr. Johnson's definition of port wine: "Why, gentlemen, it is black, it is thick, and it makes you drunk. What more do you want?" Blackguards enough you will meet in your career. Let this be our distinction, that the absence of the blackguard in politics marks the presence of the Alpha Delta Phi.

There is one other way in which we may serve our politics, and that is in never being afraid to stand alone or in the minority. A man is not necessarily right because he is in the minority, but remember that every great movement begins with a minority. It is not the child of the Medici lounging in the frescoed corridors of the Vatican, lapped in all the luxury of ecclesiastical pomp, and infallibly supreme, from whom we anticipate the impulse of religious purification and progress, but from some solitary monk in scholastic seclusion, whose first faint word is like the earliest glimmer of a spark in universal gloom, that deepens on into the noontide glory of the religious liberty in which we live. When Garrison began, the mayor of Boston, the curled darling of Faneuil Hall, wrote: "I have ferreted out the paper and its editor. His office is in an obscure hole, his only visible auxiliary is a black boy, his only known supporters are a few insignificant persons of all kinds and colors." Yes, your honor, yes; " but give me a place on which to stand," said Archimedes, " and I will move the world." In an obscure hole Garrison rested his moral lever and lifted and heaved the opinion of the continent.

Gentlemen, the majority rightfully governs, the majority rightfully rules in elections and in legislation, because for those purposes there is no expedient yet devised so sure and wise. But the majority leaves this conscience of mine and those consciences of yours absolutely unruled. No man, I say, is right because he is in the minority, but a man is wrong when he fears to be in the minority. In all human progress somebody must go first. In the purification and elevation of American politics let Alpha Delta Phi lead. This is the spirit of our Fraternity. What else has been the spirit which was not only unfolded to us in the glowing eloquence of the morning's discourse, but which has invested the life and the career of our orator with an unfading lustre? Fifty years ago another scholar at another college—and the words were recalled to me as

I listened this morning—reproducing in our own literature, in our own matchless prose, the very thought of Schiller in Don Carlos, which the orator quoted—Ralph Waldo Emerson said to the graduates of Dartmouth as they left its doors : " When you shall say, as others do so must I, I renounce, I am sorry for it, the dreams of my youth, I must eat the fat of the land and let learning and romantic inspiration go until a more convenient season, then dies the man in you, then perish the buds of art, of poetry, of science, as they have died already in a thousand, thousand men. The hour of that choice is the crisis of your history. See to it that you hold yourself fast by the intellect."

What else, gentlemen, was the spirit of him, our brother, whom we had hoped to see with us this evening, and whose death is like the sudden extinction of a pure and bright light by which men were guiding their footsteps? Of late years I have seen little of Dr. Hitchcock, but that same simplicity and earnestness, that same broad sympathy and charity and kindly humor, that vigorous and vigilant mind, that glowing heart and burning word of patriotism which lifted and held and strengthened men in our great national controversy—all these I knew when wandering with him in other lands in other summers when the days were long. But that inflexible constancy, that moral independence, that modesty, that urbanity, that uncompromising fidelity to duty, let them be not only the glory of our friend and teacher, let them be also a tie of Alpha Delta Phi. "Where flies the white plume of Navarre," said the old French poet, "there follows victory!" And how shall we serve our mother so well, how so truly approve ourselves her children, how so surely make her countenance radiant to all beholders, as by forcing the cry, where honor and honesty appear in politics, "There rides Alpha Delta Phi and Victory at her side!"

FIFTY YEARS OF AMERICAN SCHOLARSHIP.

WILLIAM HAYES WARD, D.D., LL.D., '56.

During the fifty years since our loved fraternity was introduced to this loved college there has been nothing less than a revolution in the aims and methods of American scholarship, and in this revolution our own members have had their noble part. Scholarship used to be—I hope it still is—the chief test by which were gauged the young candidates for initiation. We aimed for good scholars, men ambitious of honestly doing what they came here professedly to do. No other one thing would tell so well what was their calibre and what their executive power. Out of such men we would get some leaders.

Our country has now fairly entered upon the second stage of her scholastic history. The first period was a long one, that of reception. Our best scholars were little other than school-boys. They learned what others had put in books, and even the books were few. Dr. Wayland said forty years ago that there were not the books in this country to allow the production of a thoroughly scholarly treatise. Our fathers had scarcely the materials or the incitements to devote themselves to the higher tasks of original scholarship. What had descended to them, what other scholars had discovered and written down, these men taught, so far as they found it, to their pupils. They taught them to do what they had done, to receive and retain, and nothing more.

Of course there were some noble exceptions to this rule, but it was a general one. But besides such sporadic exceptions there was in the history of American scholarship just one grand exception, and that was in theology. New England was settled by the most independent thinkers in theology of their day, and the breed has never become extinct. Every generation has had its freshened theology. The younger Edwards enumerated ten points in which his father had made what he called "Improvements in Theology," and he straightway proceeds to add to their number. It is not the Edward A. Park and the Egbert C. Smyth of our generation alone that we must honor for their productive as well as receptive power, but before them Taylor and Emmons and Hopkins and Bellamy, and chief among them the greatest factor in theologic progress which this country has yet seen, President Edwards. When I speak of a revolution in scholarship in our own days, I expressly exclude theology, a science peculiarly American.

The second stage in the history of American scholarship is the productive. We have begun to learn to increase and not simply to preserve knowledge. Thereby we pass out of the eddy into the current. A study of Chinese art and science is worthless. It shows us a path lost in the sands. Those little-headed people had a feminine power of worshiping their ancestors and retaining what they had given. But they had not the masculine power of striking out anything new. If you want to study productive and useful history, you must follow the widening current, beginning at the fountain-head of art and learning on the shore of the Persian Gulf, where Nimrod fought the wild bulls about Eridu the

Blessed; then going north a little to old Sippara, where the Chaldean historian tells us that Noah buried the records of the antediluvian world, and from which he dug them up after the Flood; then north again to Assyria; thence westward through old Carchemish and the Hittite Kingdom to the Sidonian shore; then along the coast and islands inhabited by awakening Hellenic tribes, Sardis, Smyrna and Cyprus, till we reach glorious Greece, in whose development it seemed for a while that we had attained the highest possible ridge of progress and could go no higher. But then, after some centuries of rest, there came in a new moral force from Judea, which, taken up at last, with the scientific principles of Aristotle, into the blood of fresh nations, produced, through Italian and Teutonic and Norman races, the marvel of modern industrial and scientific, helpful, progressive and productive civilization. Only within the last few years has America got fairly into the current of this progress and begun to add to its force.

It was natural that the new era should begin with science. Geology led the way, under the impulse of two great men,

Benjamin Silliman, of Yale, and Edward Hitchcock, of Amherst. The latter we claim as one of our brothers, born out of due time; but his sons, are they not ours by true birth? A little later Torrey and Gray became the fathers of American botany. Most important of the natural sciences, biology did not exist until Agassiz was imported to teach in Harvard College. But that great teacher left behind him a great company of enthusiastic pupils, each more advanced than he. Now there is no department of the natural sciences, unless it be, possibly, chemistry, in which we need feel ashamed of our record by the side of that of England, Germany or France. Not one of those nations possesses to-day more active, original investigators than Hall, Hayden, Dana, Leconte, Marsh, Cope and a dozen others, who could be mentioned in geology and palæontology; than Gray, Wilder, Coues, Verrill and the younger Agassiz in biology; than Newcomb, Peters, Holden, Young, Gould, Langley, Newton and Asaph Hall in astronomy; or than Rutherfurd, Rowland, Bell and Edison in physics.

Linguistics owes a mighty debt to two American scholars, the one of them,

William D. Whitney, of Yale, and the other, Francis A. March, of Lafayette. The one is the father of all them that study Sanscrit, and the other of all them that love the Anglo-Saxon and the early English. The latter we are proud to honor as a brother of our chapter. There is no more vigorous school of Sanscritists in the world than those that call Whitney their father; and among them no one has done more honorable original work than he who is, perhaps, the oldest of them, our own Amherst brother—Professor Avery, of Bowdoin College. We congratulate the other institutions that have got so many of our great scholars. Professor March's pupils, who have taken up the history of European languages, are younger men, but we shall hear from them.

The study of the other oriental languages is yet more recent with us. Twenty-five years ago Hebrew was taught in a dreamy way in fifty seminaries, perhaps, and nothing was known of it. It was a Pennsylvania German theological professor who spoke of Hebrew as that tongue which he had *siebenmal gelernt und siebenmal vergessen.* Yale had one man semi-attached to it who was understood to understand Arabic; but less than ten years ago, when a student at Harvard handed in a thesis on Arabic studies with a view to the Ph.D. degree, there was no one in Cambridge who could pass on it, and it had to be sent to the aged secretary of the Oriental Society at New Haven. Now we have not only our summer schools of Hebrew, where all the Semitic languages are taught to everybody, but within these last ten years, not to say five years, our theological seminaries have been manned with active and productive Hebraists; at least three men are at work in original Syriac investigation, editing new texts, and Assyrian is taught by competent young men in half a dozen institutions, while creditable additions have been made by Lyon, Smith and others, to our knowledge of Assyrian literature and art. We are yet behind in some things—no one knows anything of Egyptology—but in no country is the promise better. There are many more students of Assyrian in America than in England or France—more than in Germany.

Let me say a word of the latest of the sciences, Sociology, from which we cannot disconnect history and the science of government. I honor the men who, outside the schools, under the impulse of the old political economy or of mere politics, have made their studies of imposts and tariffs —such men as Carey, and Atkinson, and Henry George. But within a very few years a new science of public affairs has risen, and on a more scientific and inductive basis. It is yet in an inchoate condition. It is yet feeling about for its facts and has not wholly found out its principles. It does not yet *quite* know whether it is a science of selfishness or of altruism. In this work the schools have led the way— Columbia, Johns Hopkins, Cornell, and last, Harvard and Yale. All these universities have fine departments of political science, and they publish two quarterly journals than which nothing better appears in Europe. It is only just to say that one of our Amherst brothers, Professor Burgess, of Columbia College, has been more than any other man the leader of this new movement. The fate that took him from Amherst College I have mourned more than any other misfortune the college has met since I have known it. Out of what other influence like his came that troop of young men that had awakened in them the true scholar's ambition, and that flocked to Germany and to our own new Johns Hopkins that they might learn not only how to learn but how to produce? He has found, perhaps, a wider field there than he could have found here, although as I look over the list of the editors of those projected cyclopedias of sociological science that are so soon to come out under the editorship of Professor Burgess and his associates, and find six out of nine of them prepared by Amherst men, I wonder if Amherst College has been moved to New York.

The history of the new development of American scholarship is the story of a few great teachers—Silliman, Hitchcock, Gray, Agassiz, Whitney, March, Burgess. It expressed itself in the founding of Johns Hopkins University, and the annexing of true postgraduate university departments to Yale, Harvard and Columbia, and latest Princeton, colleges.

We see the fruit of it in our chairs of instruction, where no man can now expect to get a position who has not studied abroad, and who cannot talk German and French and perhaps modern Greek (not yet Latin, alas!) as well as English. He must be a citizen of the world and acquainted with all that the great Republic of Letters is doing. That is not now the best college which teaches best how to acquire the old learning, but that which inspires most the noble ambition of adding something to the world's stock of useful knowledge — that ambition which is most akin to the Christian ambition to increase the store of the world's goodness and happiness. The review of the period covered by the history of our chapter surprises me as I see how large a part this fraternity has had in this American renaissance. Perhaps there has been something in the spirit of our order that has been in touch with the best spirit of the age, and has taught us that they best serve God and men who can lead in the van.

THE FRATERNITY OF ALPHA DELTA PHI.

HON. JOSEPH H. CHOATE, *Harvard, '52*.
PRESIDENT OF THE FRATERNITY.

Mr. President and Brethren, and may I not also say Sisters of Alpha Delta Phi:

The average Amherst brain must be very elastic. We have always known that the true Alpha Delt's cranium is insatiable and inexhaustible, but after the experience of the last twenty-four hours it seems to me that the moment has come to cry a halt. My poor brain will hold no more, and I should deem myself guilty of an outrage indeed if I undertook to add one serious thought to the terrible load which has been imposed upon you since the sun rose to-day. Just think of it! The Ivy oration, that peerless oration of Dr. Storrs, which has excited the admiration, the envy and the applause of this community; the Grove oration, I believe they call it, and the six or seven orations which have now been delivered in your presence. I therefore refuse to say one serious word, and I propose to devote the five minutes allotted to me, as the President of this Fraternity, in speaking without saying anything, which, I believe, has always been recognized as the true merit and art of after-dinner speaking. But before I proceed to speak on the toast assigned me, it seems to me that I ought, at least, to attempt to vindicate the much abused character of a brother of the Harvard chapter, the only brother, I believe, in this vast assembly to-day representing that time-honored chapter. That was the unkindest cut of all this morning. With all the beauty of Amherst before him, and all its manliness behind him, for this peerless orator of the day to cast such obloquy upon the Harvard brother!

Now, I never had the pleasure and honor of knowing Amherst before, except by traditions that had lingered in Harvard on a visit that was made to that institution nearly fifty years ago by two rustic brethren of the class of '39 from the Amherst chapter. They came to extend the blessings of the

Fraternity and to visit their far remote and somewhat cool brethren at Cambridge. They came with the hayseed of Hampshire in their hair. Their hair, from being parted in the middle, was, in fact, not parted at all. It is true they brought with them no cane, but they carried upon their shoulders the old familiar umbrella which had come down from a prehistoric period. It is true they wore no gloves, but they wore their trousers in their boots, and I need not say to you that they left an impression in the Harvard mind which has taken all the glorious demonstrations of this day to efface from the memory of their representative. Well, gentlemen, I will let the Harvard chapter speak for itself. Literature, I believe, has been the first great end and aim of Alpha Delta Phi, and if the Harvard chapter had done nothing for the Fraternity, and the world, but to give it James Russell Lowell, the Harvard chapter would rest content. In view of this unkind reflection passed upon me, and those whom I hold near and dear, by the orator of the day, I will not throw any additional laurels upon those which already crown his brow. There was one criticism on his oration, however, which did strike me with great interest and delight. It was that which he received before he had said a word. His reputation had drawn to the body of the house all that was manly and learned and strong in the surroundings of Amherst. It had attracted to the gallery all the women that sympathize with Alpha Delta Phi—and what true woman does not?—and not only the women, but the babies too. And when he unrolled and laid upon the desk that copious and ponderous manuscript from which he was to speak, that infant cry from the North convulsed my heart. Who was that youthful stranger? You have heard of the kinship of Alpha Delta Phi, he was the son of a true Alpha Delt. He was precocious, audacious, it was true. He had come to hear the oration, but when he saw that grand manuscript unfolded, he said to himself and to his mother, "This is too much," and he retired before a single blow was dealt. He retired in dismay, because, however much he may grow to the stature of the perfect Alpha Delt, he saw that that was not milk for babies, but strong meat for men.

Now, in my service as President of this

Fraternity, I have been very much struck with some things. As I have attended the convention at New York, at Ithaca, at Boston, and at Amherst at last, the presence of women in our deliberations and at our festivities has struck me with interest and admiration. Co-education, as Dr. Storrs demonstrated this morning, in that close tie that binds Amherst to Northampton, is already accomplished. In the performance of my duty as President of the Fraternity it has been my pleasure to read the reports as they have come from all the undergraduate chapters, and from those where co-education was really carried into practice, I have been very much struck with one significant, harmonious, and uniform report. You know the younger brethren of all the chapters like to magnify the position and relations within their respective colleges, and all these uniformly report that "the highest honor in our college has been carried off by a woman, but the best *man* is an Alpha Delt."

Now, I know of no remedy for this state of things but that we admit them into full fraternity. By and by we shall have a chapter of sisters who will come up with the star and crescent upon their breasts. I echo the fine oration on the chivalry of Alpha Delta Phi: When our sisters so come, they will be received by the brethren with open hearts, and arms extended wide.

Now of the Fraternity and of my duties as President of the association. It has been happily compared by Mr. Curtis — the office of President of this Fraternity — with that of the President of the United States. There is much in common between the two dignified positions. In the first place, there is but one man among the sixty millions of American citizens who can occupy the position at the same time. In the second place, the salary of the President is, I believe, altogether inadequate to the great duties he has to perform. I have found it almost necessary to abandon my usual calling and give myself up to its duties. Journeys to Ithaca, journeys to Boston, journeys to Amherst—all richly repaid by that grand feast of reason that I found there—but none of the usual material profit. And I found another thing —Mr. Curtis will correct me if I am wrong, for he knows who said that the real avenue to his brain is through the stomach ; so your

President has found that it has been necessary for that organ to be cultivated so to enable him to perform the duties pertaining to the office. We sat down to a banquet beginning at one o'clock in the morning, and at Boston we sat nearly until daylight. Here there is one feature which certainly has not been tried, however inspiring it is —it is the first Alpha Delta Phi banquet that I have ever attended which is on the true prohibition temperance style. However much that may impair our digestion, it appeals to our patriotism, to our sense of duty as good citizens.

I have not been entirely satisfied with the review of the last fifty years of Alpha Delta Phi. It does seem to me that sufficient credit has not been claimed for the achievements of the Fraternity. When you compare the benighted condition of mankind as it was before this Fraternity was established, with what it is to-day, in every realm of human interest and human knowledge and human character, how infinite is the debt which the world owes to the founders of this Fraternity. I claim the credit of all the great things that have been done as the immediate and direct result of the foundation of this society and its development in the last fifty years. Mr. Curtis has said a great deal about Alpha Delta Phi in politics. He has given you something in the abstract. This society has given to the world something in the concrete. When you consider the great reform that is now going on in American politics and American public life, when you look for the men who have done the most to put an end to the corruption and incompetency in office, to make it a real fact that public office is only a public duty and a public trust, who are the men to whom the world may well point as chief factors in the result? Does not the first and foremost sit beside me at this table. And when you look for his coadjutors in that great service, where will you find the names of men who have done more to uphold his hands than our brothers Everett P. Wheeler and Charles F. Fairchild, who now occupies the post of the Secretary of the Treasury.

But I am afraid I am getting serious. I did not intend it, I never meant to, and I must apologize for it. There is one idea which seems worth drawing out, that is the advancing of this great cause of the promotion of the civil service. Inasmuch as these three brothers of ours have done so well, why would it not be a good plan to extend the service throughout all the branches of this Fraternity? In these days there is no distinction that is discernible between a member of one party that exists and a member of the other. Why would it not be a good plan, Mr. President and brethren, to form a new party upon this platform; that the public service in all its branches should be entrusted to the members of Alpha Delta Phi? We would know then that every public duty would be well performed. It is true there are not enough to fill all the offices, but 6,000 members of this Fraternity would fill all the principal ones—all that were worth having, or that were acceptable. That is something that I would throw out for the consideration of the representatives of the various chapters to contemplate and act upon.

Mr. President, a word has been said by President Seelye of the good influence that this Fraternity has exercised in the various colleges of the land. But I do not think, after all, that we can claim all of the credit of civilization as it exists to-day. I did think so once. I do not know the true merits of the case which he presents, but last winter, in my honored capacity as President of this Fraternity, I received a most striking compliment. That society which has stood side by side and shoulder to shoulder with ours in all the various colleges of the land, celebrated in New York the 50th anniversary of its birth, and I was invited, as your representative, to a seat at their board. It was the first time that any encroachment had been made upon those barriers of separation and hostility which had so long divided that association from ours. You may imagine what a telling sermon I was able to preach to them, reviewing our careers, the rivalry of emulation, of actual hostility at times, pointing out to them how they had warred upon us with relentless fury in all the colleges. I took for my text one that they fully appreciated: "Love your enemies; bless them that curse you; do good to them that despitefully use you."

Now, brethren, I am sorry for you—you have to listen to eight more orations and I fear you will have to sit here until two or three in the morning until all the orators have had their say. I trust you will all survive. I trust the members now present will be able to come down to New York about the month of May next and show no worse for the torrents of oratory and floods of wisdom with which you have been overwhelmed at Amherst.

GREEK LETTERS AND LETTERS LITERARY.

PROF. F. A. MARCH, '45.

Here and now there can be only three letters to speak of, *Α Δ Φ* — emblems of friendship, of fraternity among scholars— emblems, therefore, of the deepest and richest sources of all that is best in literature. Intellect is a servant of nature, the creative power in literature. Genius springs from the affections. In college recitations and halls of debate we sharpen our wits for the battle of life. We may get to be as sharp and as smart as one of Shakespeare's fools; but it is in the cosy rooms of *Α Δ Φ*, or on summer evenings, perhaps, on the chapel steps, crooning with a brother in *Α Δ Φ*, as we sit looking westward on all the wondrous beauties of our valley, or skyward, where the crescent moon with a single star at her side reigns o'er half a heaven of blue, that those thoughts arise which make us free of the realm of beauty and truth. Here wit tempered with love becomes humor. Here knowledge steeped in the affections becomes wisdom. Here talent, new born, becomes genius.

The serene temper, the genial manner, the radiant face of a whole-souled brother of a scholar's Fraternity are "the brave complexion which leads the van and swallows up the cities."

A chapter of $A \mathit{\Delta} \Phi$ is a nursery of genial manhood, an eyrie where genius broods its wings.

BROTHERHOOD WITHIN AND WITHOUT.

HON. H. S. STOCKBRIDGE, '45.

Mr. President: The theme which you have assigned to me has been, at least in one of its departments, so thoroughly covered by our president that it seems to me, as at the Methodist meetings after the sermon, there needs only a few words. But it is due to myself that I should say, in one respect at least, I am not unlike the good old deacon, in the land of steady habits for too great an indulgence in that which inebriates more than it cheers. He said: "While I cannot deny the fact, I deny the criminality, for I have prayed that this thing might depart from me, and now I have shifted the responsibility." You are aware, Mr. President, that I endeavored and asked that I should not be imposed upon this audience; therefore I have, as the good old deacon did, shifted the responsibility.

But when we come to speak of the brotherhood within our own breasts it is a thing to be felt and not talked about. The spirit engendered in our chapter-house on yonder hill, stretching over continent and ocean, has drawn men here to this semi-centennial anniversary from all quarters of the globe, and from all vocations and pursuits of life, to review again the strongest and most lasting attachments, as well as the most cherished friendships, of their lives. I am sure no one who has been away from his chapter as long as I, has ever found any attachment in life, in friendship, so abiding as those which they formed in Alpha Delta Phi of Amherst College. I have always found members of the Alpha Delta Phi, from whatever chapter they came, true to the pledges they have assumed, ready to recognize a brother by the kindred of blood, to do him a favor on every opportunity. I have found them most entitled to the particular and marked attention and respect, not of the brotherhood alone, but of the world at large. This is the brotherhood of the Alpha Delta Phi —nobility and unselfishness of purposes, of aspirations, of aim, and it is as lasting as the lives of the men who enter into that brotherhood.

But when we speak of the brotherhood without, the gentleman who sat beside me a few minutes ago suggested the words of the apostle, "Bless them that curse you; do good to them that despitefully use you." While we do not mean to say by any means that all without are barbarians, we do mean to say that all that are without should not be kept there. Speaking of the brotherhood without, I suppose the first thing this brotherhood will embrace, as suggested by the orator of the day, is the institution across the river at Northampton. I am sure the younger members would be glad to recognize that as a branch.

But there is another thought. Looking over the world's history we find that the struggle has not been for brotherhood but for mastery. We have had the pleasure of seeing, within the last few years, that these great struggles for mastery which have bathed the world in blood and desolation, have taken a different course. We find that when the influences that control our chapter, here and elsewhere, prevail, a different way has been found of settling the world's disagreements than that one which has set them at the cannon's mouth.

Now, then, as the world progresses, and principles which we learn to inculcate prevail, we shall find, if we live until the millennium, that the brotherhood of man is that consummation, that flower of the ages, towards which all things are tending and to which brotherhoods like this more than perhaps any other thing, unless it shall be the Christian Church, shall tend to advance.

But I insist, Mr. President, considering what the president of the organization has said, that I should not inflict another word upon him or the Fraternity.

LOVE THE SISTERHOOD.

PRES. TRUMAN J. BACKUS, *Rochester*, '64.

Brothers in Alpha Delta Phi:

As I have recalled the post-prandial scenes of recent years, and reminded myself of the one sentiment usually assigned to me for a response, a train of reflection has been awakened which naturally separates into three parts : first, the men of one idea ; secondly, the men who are supposed to have but one idea ; thirdly, the one idea.

In discussing a theme so perplexing to you, so simple and familiar to me (for perplexity and simplicity are relative to thinkers), we may serve our mutual convenience by adopting the homiletical method of the negro divine whose text suggested its own division; the world, the flesh, the devil. As he did, so will we, discuss the first point briefly, touch lightly upon the second, and hasten on to the third as rapidly as possible.

The man of one idea. Hazlitt has embalmed the prototype. The progeny, however widely scattered, display the features of their lineage, are known to all men, and meet an affected and universal disapproval. But, in fact, all men admire and envy them; and every aspirant after mortal glory hopes, at some day, and soon, to lose himself in the immensity of an idea. In this concealed aspiration the man of our generation is reasonable; for this is the age of scientific research, and science is the product of analytical method, and analysis is but another name for classification, and classification evokes the specialist, and the specialist is a man of one idea —the great man of our generation.

The unthinking company at the banqueting table, refusing to hear the "crank" and "fanatic," still hail righteousness and eternal fitness in the fact that the followers of one certain calling are men of one idea.

Secondly, the men who are supposed to have but one idea. They are the presidents of colleges for women, and the masters of high schools for girls. The world seems never weary of their theme. At the public corner, and in the mystic retreat where the star never dims and the crescent never wanes, the listener appeals for sentiments from these priests of one idea.

Thirdly, the one idea.

The great idea of this generation is the higher education of women. It is bringing neatness, order, vivacity, patience, gentleness, devotion and scholarliness into the schoolrooms, and there they will abide and increase, and will develop our schools, from the lowest to the highest, until the dreams of the lovers of youth are fulfilled. It is working as leaven in our churches, assimilating dry doctrines, transmuting them into principles of righteousness, and giving them issue again in thoughtful guidance of the wayward and the poor. It is reorganizing the penitentiary, cleansing the air of hospitals, managing refuges for the Magdalen and the foundling, preaching the good news of sanitation, checking the arrogance of King Alcohol, and arraigning the maladministration of government in our cities. You, yourselves, are witnesses of the inspiring advance along these lines, made during the last twenty years. Whence the inspiration? It has come from the organized work of women. They have found their leaders; these leaders are themselves women who know the power attained by patient, methodic, mental training.

It happened that the exigencies of the Civil War summoned women to the field. They did much of the work of the Sanitary and Christian commissions. They were there learning to be active parts of gigantic organizations. They tasted the sweetness of heroism, and made it impossible for the noble of their sex to be satisfied with inactivity. It happened, also, while the war was going on, while patriotism was making the dullard ardent, and the youth serious, that Matthew Vassar, both prophet and apostle of a new idea, was raising a temple commemorative of his sympathy with the intellectual ambitions of women. When the war was over, the temple was builded, its doors were opened, and thither went the aspiring daughters of the land.

The schools of a generation ago laid but a thin film of scholarship upon young women — a cheap electroplating of ethics and æsthetics,—astronomy without mathematics, and art copied from the flat. Remind yourselves of that pretentious superficiality, and from it turn to look upon the throngs of young women climbing the steep ascents of learning, along the rugged ways which have been builded at Vassar, at Wellesley, at Smith, at Bryn Mawr, and at a score of colleges where brother and sister are panting towards the summit—the weary brother pushed along—the ambitious sister pulling at the reins—and when you have noted the contrast between the old-time "female education," and "the higher education of women," you will have recognized the force in our social life which is giving us new industries, larger education, broader philanthropy, and better administration of all public affairs.

When Mr. Vassar gave his large wealth to endow the college which bears his name, he startled America and Europe by the boldness and novelty of his philanthropy. Facetious people styled his institution "Vassar's Folly." It was an experiment. For the man of the world, the experiment was to prove whether young women in numbers sufficient to organize a college would deny themselves the pleasures of social life, and pay the time and effort demanded as the price of a scholastic degree; for the special friends of education the experiment was to decide whether the physical and the mental constitution of woman was capable of enduring the strain of an advanced and rigorous course of study. There were no other questions involved. Young women in large and ever-growing numbers seek the training offered by their colleges; and these colleges to-day are wielding one of their most beneficent influences in training their students to attain the dignity of fine physical development.

Twenty years ago the popular faith believed that there is "sex in education." Now you may transpose the courses of study at Amherst and Vassar, at Smith and Cornell, and the students will not know that they have been unsexed, nor will the professors discover that their students have lost or gained in the number of mental faculties. Then a college for women was supposed to be a seminary for sentimentalism. Now a college is admitted to be a school where advanced lines of training in mathematics, in natural and physical science, in literature and language, are given, regardless of the question whether the students find their supplementary training in boat-racing or in embroidery. The old theory of "sex in education" is stranded and abandoned.

The surprising educational achievements

of these twenty years are due, chiefly, to the earnestness of young women at college. They have demanded that there be no pretense, no substitute for a thorough and difficult curriculum. They have been in communication with young men at college, have kept themselves informed as to the kind and the degree of training given at Amherst, Harvard and Yale, and have been prompt in challenging the necessity, the wisdom, the honesty of any modification of requirements whereby the young woman might secure the easier graduation. Every college official knows the potency of the moral sentiment among students, in constraining the legislation of a college faculty; and that constraint has been operative in colleges for women, compelling their conformity to the severe course of study assigned at the highest colleges for men.

So Vassar, Smith, Wellesley have drifted from the quiet moorings selected for them by friendly theorists of twenty years ago, and have been borne along the deep channel which has been worn by the movement of two centuries of American college history. That channel has broadened, has changed its direction by slow processes, but the main channel as it runs to-day, is kept by the novel craft, a woman's college.

The sources of error regarding woman's limitations in the world of learning were near the surface. It was believed that her body could not endure the strain of a college course—an honest belief, now proved to be erroneous. Statistics offer the perfect refutation—indeed they discovered a law that the health of a young woman improves under the collegiate discipline. It is natural that this result should appear ; for, entering college, she is transferred from social life, where over-feeding and under-sleeping impair health, from the home where her wish, however injudicious, is the will of the family ; and she is brought into a life where self-respect exacts industry and conformity to regulations, where she must have constant regard for others in order that others may have regard for her, where the hours for sleep and the hours for eating are ordered by the faultless tyranny of a clock from whose decree there is no appeal. Living under such regulations, and debarred from her brother's excesses, she is usually in condition better than his for the exactions of the class-room.

There was a sentimental theory about the native intuitional power of woman—a power which was supposed to lift her above the need of advanced training, and at the same time, to disqualify her for sustaining protracted logical processes. Now, whatever a woman's intuitional gifts may be, they do not make her an idiot, they do not debar her from severe work in mathematics and psychology. For my part, I think that the talk about woman's intuition is bald nonsense, and that the facts advanced for its support are perverted. It is, doubtless, a fact that women are more ready to admit the claims of duty than are men. A man and a woman look at such a claim; the woman promptly bows to it, while the man squints, looks aside and quibbles until he is compelled to face the claim. Then he gallantly lies about the superiority of woman's intuition. All facts submitted in support of this hypocritical theory are, singularly enough, from the realm of ethics. No woman's unthinking intuition ever solved Sturm's Theorem, or translated the Preface of Livy, or detected Kant's distinction between the reason and the understanding.

There was an undertone of sentiment, deep and charming, to the effect that a woman should be a wife and a mother; but that sentiment, once advanced with potency against the collegiate education of women, has lost its significance, for a thousand experiments have proved that a woman graduated from college may be a wife and a mother.

All other solicitudes and objections were insignificant when compared with the dread men had lest collegiate education should make women masculine. You had it; so had I. How preposterous now to one who sees the intellectual refinement, the æsthetic pleasures, the social dignity of many a home made conspicuous in these charms by the graces and powers developed in the mistress of that home under the training of her college days.

We once said that young women would not give the time demanded by the college, and many people still think that they should not. But what is a young woman to do after leaving the secondary school? It is a time most critical in the forming of character. Social tyranny forbids her serving an employer. The hand of idleness will hold her hand ; and she will be of heroic mould whom idleness does not betray into flirting with things in male apparel, or forming undying loves for other women, or writing poetry. No people have so much leisure as the daughters of well-to-do parentage just when the college invites them to her shelter.

Such barren and treacherous arguments once arrayed the public sentiment against the movement favorable to the higher education of women. But all observing people have seen the futility of such objections, and concede that brother and sister have like organs of sense, have like native powers of perception and reason, and under the inexorable laws of thought, must think in the same forms of syllogistic reasoning.

The higher education of woman is the eminent social achievement of our age ; the college girls, themselves, despite popular prejudice and the inefficiency of their teachers, have achieved the victory.

Brothers in Alpha Delta Phi, how full of chivalry and common sense are the words of our presiding officer when he summons us to " LOVE THE SISTERHOOD ! "

MEMBERSHIP OF THE CHAPTER

CHARTER MEMBERS.

Lucian Barbour	I. Z.
Edwin Elisha Bliss	N. Σ.
Whiting Griswold	B'. X'.
Nathaniel Lynds Lord	A. M.
John Alexander McKinstry	O. P.
Jonathan Bryant Marshall	O. T.
Horace Maynard	E'. Λ'.
Alexander Montgomery	A. T.
George Bliss Morris	P. A.
Joseph Peckham	E. B.
William Barrett Reed	A. Δ.
Daniel Rice	E. X.
Joel Edson Rockwell	E. A.
Curtis Benjamin Minor Smith	P. Γ.
James Smith Thayer	E. Δ. K.
Charles Ellery Washburn	B. Υ'.
Henry Warren Williams	P. Δ.

ADDRESS LIST.

ABBE, WILLIAM ALANSON, '57.
  New Bedford, Mass.
ABBOTT, ASA GEORGE, '65.
  Died July 2, 1870.
ADAMS, GEORGE MOULTON, REV., '44.
  Holliston, Mass.
ALDEN, EDMUND KIMBALL, REV., '44.
  1 Somerset St., Boston, Mass.
ALDEN, EDMUND KIMBALL, '80.
  "Century" Co., 33 East 17th St., New York City.
ALLEN, ADDISON, '88.
  Columbia College Law School.
ALLEN, GLENN SEVIENNE, '89.
  Amherst College, Amherst, Mass.
ALLEN, WASHINGTON IRVING, '62.
  Silver Reef, Utah.
ALVORD, ALFRED ELY, '84.
  40 Water St., Boston, Mass.
ALVORD, ANDREW PORTER, '87.
  175 Herkimer St., Brooklyn, N. Y.
AMES, HERBERT BROWN, '85.
  Care of Ames, Holden & Co., Montreal, Canada.
APPLETON, SAMUEL EDWARDS, '84.
  48 West Ninth St., New York City.
ARMSBY, LAUREN, REV., '42.
  Council Grove, Kansas.
ARMSTRONG, COLLIN, '77.
  "Sun" Office, Park Row, New York City.
ARNELL, DAVID REEVE, '40.
  Died July 25, 1852.
AUSTIN, HARMON, '88.
  Amherst College, Amherst, Mass.
AVERY, JOHN, '61.
  Brunswick, Maine.

BABBOTT, FRANK LUSK, LL.B., '78.
  13th Ave. and 25th St., New York City.
BALL, WILLIAM CREIGHTON, '68.
  Terre Haute, Ind.
BANCROFT, FREDERIC AUSTIN, '82.
  Freiburg, Baden, Germany.
BANCROFT, JACOB HENRY, REV., '39.
  Died August 25, 1844.
BARBOUR, LUCIAN, '37.
  Died
BARKER, JAMES LAWRENCE, '65.
  Santa Barbara, Cal.
BARROWS, JOHN OTTIS, REV., '60.
  Newington, Conn.
BARROWS, WILLIAM HENRY, REV., '59.
  Montour, Iowa.
BARTON, HOMER ROLLIN, '63.
  Died August 12, 1863.
BARTON, WALTER, REV., '56.
  Attleboro', Mass.
BATEMAN, CLIFFORD RUSH, '76.
  Died February 6, 1883.
BEATTIE, DAVID, '59.
  Troy, N. Y.
BEECHER, HERBERT FOOTE, '76.
  Port Townsend, Washington Territory.
BEECHER, HENRY WARD, REV., '34.
  Died March 8, 1887.
BEST, JAMES, '85.
  Kinderhook, N. Y.
BICKNELL, THOMAS WILLIAMS, '57.
  Worcester Station, Boston, Mass.
BILLINGS, CHARLES MORRIS, M.D., '63.
  Nashua, Chickasaw Co., Iowa.
BILLINGS, RICHARD SALTER, REV., '47.
  Danbury, Conn.
BISBEE, JOSEPH BARTLETT, '80.
  Poughkeepsie, N. Y.
BISHOP, GEORGE SAYLES, REV., '58.
  14 Burnet St., East Orange, N. J.

BISHOP, JAMES LORD, LL.B., '65.
 115 Broadway, New York City.
BLAKE, LUCIEN IRA, Ph.D., '77.
 Rose Polytechnic, Terre Haute, Ind.
BLAKE, MAURICE BENAIAH, '66.
 Died February 8, 1886.
BLANCHARD, JOSEPH NATHANIEL, REV., '71.
 St. John's Rectory, Detroit, Mich.
BLATCHFORD, PAUL, '82.
 375 La Salle Ave., Chicago, Ill.
BLISS, CHARLES LINCOLN, '88.
 Amherst College, Amherst, Mass.
BLISS, EDWIN ELISHA, REV., '37.
 Newton Centre, Mass.
BLISS, EDWIN MUNSELL, REV., '71.
 Bible House, Constantinople, Turkey.
BLISS, FREDERICK JONES, REV., '80.
 Amherst, Mass.
BLISS, HOWARD SWEETZER, REV., '82.
 Amherst, Mass.
BLISS, WILLIAM DWIGHT PORTER, '78.
 Lee, Mass.
BLISS, WILLIAM TYLER, '87.
 32 Halsted St., East Orange, N. J.
BOARDMAN, JOSEPH, REV., '55.
 Barnet, Vermont.
BOLTWOOD, HENRY LEONIDAS, REV., '53.
 Evanston, Ill.
BOND, EPHRAIM WARD, LL.B., '41.
 Springfield, Mass.
BOND, NELSON FREEMAN, '64.
 Fitchburg, Mass.
BOWLER, FRANK, REV., '76.
 Grand Rapids, Mich.
BOYDEN, ARTHUR CLARKE, '76.
 State Normal School, Bridgewater, Mass.
BOYDEN WALLACE CLARKE, '83.
 Easthampton, Mass.
BRACKETT, GILBERT ROBBINS, REV., '57.
 8 Wragg St., Charleston, S. C.

BRADLEY, LEVERETT, REV., '73.
  Andover, Mass.
BRANSCOMBE, CHARLES HENRY, '45.
  Topeka, Kansas.
BRAYTON, EDMUND CULLEN, M.D., '67.
  Died September 7, 1875.
BRAYTON, GEORGE, REV., '66.
  Died June 9, 1873.
BREED, BOWMAN BIGELOW, M.D., '53.
  Died December 16, 1873.
BREED, DANIEL HENRY, '57.
  Died December 13, 1885.
BREWSTER, WILLIAM LEWIS, '88.
  Amherst College, Amherst, Mass.
BRIGHAM, DON FERDINAND, '63.
  114 Wooster St., Hartford, Conn.
BRIGHAM, JEROME RIPLEY, '45.
  525 Cass St., Milwaukee, Wis.
BROOKE, EDWIN ATLEE, '46.
  Bradford, Pa.
BROOKS, CHARLES GROSVENOR, M.D., '68.
  1 Saratoga Place, East Boston, Mass.
BROOKS, STEPHEN DRIVER, M.D., '75.
  Evansville, Ind.
BROUGHTON, NATHANIEL HOOPER, REV., '47.
  Died June 2, 1866.
BROWN, SAMUEL EDWARD, '55.
  10 Burling Slip, New York City.
BROWNELL, CHARLES HENRY, '71.
  Peru, Ind.
BROWNELL, WILLIAM CRARY, '71.
  205 West 56th St., New York City.
BUCHANAN, ABNER THOMAS, M.D., '68.
  204 North Third St., St. Louis, Mo.
BUCK, CHARLES WENTWORTH, REV., '55.
  Cambridge, Mass.
BUFFUM, CHARLES ALBERT, '75.
  Williston Seminary, Easthampton, Mass.
BURGESS, EBENEZER PRINCE, M.D., '52.
  Died May 14, 1877.

BURGESS, JOHN WILLIAM, '67.
  323 West 57th St., New York City.
BURLEY, CLARENCE AUGUSTUS (Burleigh), '72.
  Room 824, 112 Clark St., Chicago, Ill.
BURNETTE, FRANCIS ELLSWORTH, '67.
  Reed's Ferry, N. H.
BURNHAM, MICHAEL, REV., '67.
  85 Elliott St., Springfield, Mass.
BURR, CHARLES WOLCOTT, '90.
  Auburndale, Mass.
BURT, FRANCIS, '57.
  Died September 9, 1863.
BUTLER, SAMUEL PATTERSON, '71.
  "Herald" Office, Park Row, New York City.
CARSON, FRANK MARTIN, REV., '79.
  Matteawan, N. Y.
CHANCELLOR, WILLIAM ESTABROOK, '89.
  Amherst College, Amherst, Mass.
CHAPIN, FRANKLIN PERRY, REV., '52.
  Easton, Mass.
CHAPIN, GEORGE MOOAR, '79.
  16 Montauk Block, Chicago, Ill.
CHAPIN, LUCIUS DELISON, REV., '51.
  Hyde Park, Ill.
CHAPIN, WALLACE TORRY, '87.
  Hyde Park, Ill.
CHEAVENS, HENRY MARTYN, M.D., '52.
  Ashland, Boone Co., Mo.
CHICKERING, WILLIAM HENRY, LL.B., '71.
  206 Sansome St., San Francisco, Cal.
CHILD, CHARLES JESSE, '84.
  American Legation, Bangkok, Siam,
              or Richmond, Mo.
CHOATE, RUFUS, JR., '55.
  Died January 15, 1866.
CHOATE, WASHINGTON, REV., '70.
  Irvington, N. Y.
CHURCH, GEORGE EVERETT, '72.
  Oxford Grammar School, Providence, R. I.
CLAFLIN, JAMES FITZGERALD, '59.
  262 Ashland Boulevard, Chicago, Ill.

CLAFLIN, WILLIAM, '83.
   154 Lake St., Chicago, Ill.
CLAPP, ALFRED DWIGHT, '65.
   Died November 22, 1863.
CLAPP, DEXTER, REV., '39.
   Died July 27, 1868.
CLAPP, WALTER CLAYTON, '83.
   118 West 129th St., New York City.
CLARK, ALFRED HASTINGS, '86.
   46 New York Ave., Brooklyn, N. Y.
CLARK, JEFFERSON, LL.B., '67.
   32 Nassau St., New York City.
CLARK, JOSEPH BOURNE, REV., '58.
   36 Bible House, New York City.
CLARK, ROBERT BRUCE, REV., '76.
   Goshen, N. Y.
CLARK, WILLIAM BREWSTER, M.D., '76.
   50 East 31st St., New York City.
CLARK, WILLIAM BULLOCK, '84.
   Brattleboro', Vt.
COATES, HALLAM FREER, '86.
   Alliance, Ohio.
COBURN, EDWIN, '41.
   Died in 1867.
COMSTOCK, EDWARD, '61.
   Rome, N.Y.
COOK, ROSWELL DICKINSON, '43.
   Died June 9, 1842.
COOLEY, NOAH SAXTON, '66.
   Windsor Locks, Conn.
COOLEY, ORRIN, M.D., '65.
   Died January 7, 1877.
COOMBS, ZELOTES, W., '88.
   Amherst College, Amherst, Mass.
COPELAND, GEORGE WARREN, '56.
   Malden, Mass.
CORNISH, AARON SPOONER, '68.
   21 North Market St., Boston, Mass.
COWAN, PEREZ DICKINSON, REV., '66.
   Wellesley, Mass.

CRANE, WHITING SANFORD, '64.
  88 Perry St., Detroit, Mich.
CRAWFORD, SIDNEY, REV., '61.
  Tampa, Florida.
CRAWFORD, WILLIAM, REV., '57.
  Sparta, Wis.
CRITTENDEN, WILLIAM BACON, '78.
  Bucyrus, Ohio.
CRITTENDEN, WALTER HAYDEN, '81.
  206 Broadway, New York City.
CROCKETT, GEORGE KIMBALL, '40.
  Died January 4, 1879.
CROWELL, EDWARD PAYSON, '53.
  Amherst, Mass.
CURTIS, JOSEPH SEAVER, '51.
  Died May 15, 1878.
CUTLER, SANFORD LYMAN, '85.
  Groton, Mass.
DAMON, FRANK WILLIAMS, '73.
  Honolulu, Oahu, Hawaiian Islands.
DANE, MYRON BENJAMIN, '70.
  Died October 12, 1870.
DARLING, CHARLES ROSS, LL.B., '74.
  West Publishing Co., St. Paul, Minn.
DARLING, EDWARD PARRY, '51.
  38 River St., Wilkesbarre, Pa.
DARLING, HENRY, REV., '42.
  Hamilton College, Clinton, Oneida, Co., N. Y.
DAVIS, WILLIAM VAIL WILSON, REV., '73.
  Worcester, Mass.
DELABARRE, EDMUND BURKE, '86.
  Conway, Mass.
DELABARRE, FRANK ALEXANDER, '90.
  Amherst College, Amherst, Mass.
DELANO, HENRY GILES, '58.
  Died February 19, 1859.
DELANO, CHARLES, '40.
  Died January 23, 1883.
DENISON, GEORGE, '55.
  517½ Chestnut St., St. Louis, Mo.

DERBY, HASKET, M.D., '55.
　350 Beacon St., Boston, Mass.
DICKINSON, CORNELIUS EVARTS, REV., '60.
　Marietta, Ohio.
DICKINSON, EDWARD, '84.
　Lock Box 108, Amherst, Mass.
DICKINSON, RICHARD SALTER STORRS, REV.
　'44.　Died August 28, 1856.
DICKINSON, WILLIAM AUSTIN, LL.B., '50.
　Amherst, Mass.
DICKINSON, WILLIAM COWPER, REV., '48.
　College Hill, Ohio.
DICKINSON, WILLIAM EASTMAN, REV., '55.
　Chicopee, Mass.
DIKE, SAMUEL JOHNSON, '66.
　5 East 22d St., New York City.
DONALD, ELIJAH WINCHESTER, REV., '69.
　7 West 10th St., New York City.
DOW, FRANK FOWLER, M.D., '74.
　43 South Ave., Rochester, N. Y.
DRURY, LEANDER MUZZY, '41.
　Canandaigua, N. Y.
DUDLEY, JOHN LANGDON, REV., '44.
　230 Martin St., Milwaukee, Wis.
DUFFY, EDWIN, '90.
　Amherst College, Amherst, Mass.
EDDY, THOMAS JAMES, '77.
　Fall River, Mass.
ELY, ALFRED, LL.B., '74.
　29 Nassau St., New York City.
ELY, WILLIAM BREWSTER, REV., '75.
　Died May 11, 1880.
EMERSON, BENJAMIN KENDALL, '65.
　Amherst, Mass.
EMERSON, CHARLES, '38.
　Died May 27, 1845.
EMERSON, JOHN MILTON, '49.
　Died August 3, 1869.
EMMONS, HENRY VAUGHAN, REV., '54.
　Oxford, Me.

FAIRBANKS, FRANCIS JOEL, REV., '62.
　Amherst, Mass.
FAIRBANKS, JOSEPH WHITCOMB, '66.
　16 Summit Ave., St. Paul, Minn.
FALLOWS, EDWARD HUNTINGTON, '86.
　Box 462, Exeter, N. H.
FIELD, LEVI ALPHEUS, REV., '46.
　Died October 22, 1859.
FIELD, WALTER TAYLOR, '83.
　Hyde Park P. O., Chicago, Ill.
FISKE, ARTHUR SEVERANCE, '84.
　499 La Salle Ave., Chicago, Ill.
FISKE, ASA SEVERANCE, REV., '55.
　Ithaca, N. Y.
FISKE, DANIEL TAGGART, REV., '42.
　Newburyport, Mass.
FISKE, GEORGE FOSTER, M.D., '81.
　499 La Salle Ave., Chicago, Ill.
FISKE, SAMUEL, REV., '48.
　Died May 22, 1864.
FLEMING, LOUIS ISIDORE, 47.
　Jacksonville, Fla.
FLICHTNER, GEORGE FREDERIC, REV., '67.
　Montrose, South Orange, N. J.
FOLGER, HENRY CLAY, JR., LL.B., '79.
　26 Broadway, New York City.
FOWLER, CHARLES CHAUNCEY, '51.
　Died October 28, 1876.
FOWLER, WILLIAM WORTHINGTON, '54.
　Died September 18, 1881.
FRENCH, CHARLES BROWN, '86.
　1123 Hennepin Ave,
　　　or 8 South 11th St., Minneapolis, Minn.
FRENCH, JOHN, M.D., '66.
　Died August 24, 1879.
FRENCH, JAMES PAULUS, '59.
　Died January 13, 1867.
FRENCH, SOLON TENNEY, '72.
　103 S. Clark St., Chicago, Ill.
FRENCH, STEWART WHITNEY, '89.
　Amherst College, Amherst, Mass.

FRENCH, THEODORE FRANCIS, '49.
    Died September 21, 1865.
FRISBIE, ALVAH LILLIE, REV., '57.
    Des Moines, Iowa.
FULLER, HORACE SMITH, M.D., '58.
    Hartford Conn.
GAGE, NEHEMIAH HUTCHINSON, '66.
    Died July 1, 1866.
GARDNER, GEORGE ENOS, '85.
    Room 103, 405 Main St.,
        or 60 Coral St., Worcester, Mass.
GARDNER, WILLIAM, '84.
    46 Brown Hall, Princeton, N. J.
GATES, HERBERT WRIGHT, '90.
    Amherst College, Amherst, Mass.
GAY, EDWARD, '56.
    55 Kilby St., Boston, Mass.
GILLETT, ARTHUR LINCOLN, REV., '80.
    Grand Forks, Dak.
GILLETT, EDWARD BATES, '39.
    Westfield, Mass.
GILLETT, FREDERICK HUNTINGTON,
    LL.B., '74.   Springfield, Mass.
GLADDEN, FREDERICK COHOON, '85.
    Birmingham, Ala.
GLEASON, WILLIAM STANTON, M.D., '85.
    Workhouse Hospital, Blackwell's Island, N. Y.
GODDARD, WILLIAM HENRY, '59.
    Montrose, Dak.
GOLDTHWAIT, WILLIAM COLTON, '39.
    Died November 18, 1882.
GOODRICH, GEORGE DICKINSON, REV., '53.
    Died July 26, 1870.
GOODMAN, RICHARD, JR., LL.B., '69.
    Lenox, Mass.
GOODRICH, WILLIAM WINTON, LL.B., '52.
    59 Wall St., New York City.
GOODWIN, FRANK JUDSON, '84.
    51 East 69th St., New York City.
GOOLD, CHARLES BURTON, '79.
    135 Eagle St., Albany, N. Y.

GORDON, HENRY EVARTS, '79.
    Trinidad, Col.
GOULD, GEORGE HENRY, REV., '50.
    Worcester, Mass.
GRAVES, JOHN LONG, '55.
    P. O. Box 1698, Boston, Mass.
GRAVES, SAMUEL LAWRENCE, '70.
    Fitchburg, Mass.
GRAVES, THADDEUS, '56.
    Hatfield, Mass.
GRAY, GEORGE DICKMAN, '65.
    10 California St., San Francisco, Cal.
GRAY, JOSEPH CONVERSE, LL.B., '77.
    Rooms 71 and 72, 23 Court St., Boston, Mass.
GREENE, FREDERIC WILLIAM, REV., '82.
    Andover, Mass.
GREENE, JOHN MORTON, REV., '53.
    Lowell, Mass.
GRISWOLD, WHITING, '38.
    Died October 28, 1874.
GROSVENOR, GEORGE SUMNER, '58.
    Trenton, N. J.
HALL, GEORGE CYRIL, '71.
    161 La Salle St., Chicago, Ill.
HALL, GORDON ROBERT, M.D., '72.
    266 Clinton St., Brooklyn, N. Y.
HALL, LYMAN BEECHER, '73.
    1630 Chestnut St., Philadelphia, Pa.
HAMILTON, CHARLES WOODMAN, '83.
    298 E. Water St., Milwaukee, Wis.
HAMILTON, HENRY HARRISON, REV., '68.
    Hinsdale, N. H.
HAMILTON, JOHN ALEXANDER, REV., '53.
    Congregational House, Boston, Mass.
HAMLIN, ALFRED DWIGHT FOSTER, '75.
    138 East 40th St., New York City.
HAMMOND, CHARLES, REV., '44.
    Died November 7, 1878.
HANNAFORD, DAVID OSHEAL, '52.
    Died January 19, 1861.

HARDY, ASA STRONG, '61.
  Unionville, Lake Co., Ohio.
HARDY, JACOB, '50.
  Koloa, Kauai, Hawaiian Islands.
HARRINGTON, BRAINERD TIMOTHY, '52.
  Westchester, N. Y.
HARRINGTON, NATHAN, LL.B., '64.
  Toledo, Ohio.
HARRINGTON, SAMUEL, '62.
  27 Bowdoin St., Boston, Mass.
HARRINGTON, THOMAS BALLARD, '49.
  Died February 16, 1861.
HARRIS, AUSTIN, '63.
  East Machias, Me.
HARRIS, GEORGE, JR., REV., '66.
  Andover, Mass.
HASKELL, PLINY NELSON, LL.B., '71.
  444 W. Washington St., Chicago, Ill.
HASTINGS, ROBERT WORTHINGTON, '88.
  Amherst College, Amherst, Mass.
HAYWARD, CHARLES CAPEN, '42.
  Spring Garden St., Dorchester District, Boston, Mass.
HAYWARD, JAMES, LL.B., '73.
  Hannibal, Mo.
HEAP, ARNOLD NELSON, LL.B., '73.
  95 and 97 Washington St., Chicago, Ill.
HEWIT, AUGUSTINE FRANCIS, REV., '39.
  St. Paul's Church, 9th Ave. and 59th St., New York.
HILTON, GEORGE PORTER, '81.
  Hilton Bridge Co., Albany, N. Y.
HITCHCOCK, BRADFORD WASHBURN, LL.B., '81.   44 West 20th St., New York City.
HITCHCOCK, CHARLES HENRY, '56.
  Hanover, N. H.
HITCHCOCK, EDWARD, REV., '45.
  Died February 27, 1864.
HITCHCOCK, EDWARD, M.D., '49.
  Amherst, Mass.
HITCHCOCK, EDWARD, JR., M.D., '78.
  Ithaca, N. Y.

HITCHCOCK, JOHN SAWYER, '89.
  Amherst College, Amherst, Mass.
HITCHCOCK, ROSWELL DWIGHT, REV., '36.
  Died June 16, 1887.
HOBBIE, JOHN REMINGTON, M.D., '73.
  219 East 17th St., New York City.
HOBBIE, WILLIAM ROSCOE, '69.
  Greenwich, N. Y.
HOLBROOK, DAVID LEVERETT, REV., '72.
  Lake Geneva, Wis.
HOLMES, HENRY MARTYN, REV., '60.
  Meriden, N. H., or Ayer, Mass.
HOMES, FRANCIS, REV., '48.
  Easton, Cochesset P. O., Mass.
HOWARD, CHARLES SAMUEL, '80.
  712 Greenwich St., San Francisco, Cal.
HOWELL, LUTHER CLARK, '64.
  Died October 16, 1866.
HOWLAND, GEORGE, '50.
  1420 Wabash Ave., Chicago, Ill.
HOWLAND, WALTER MORTON, '63.
  57 Portland Block, Chicago, Ill.
HOWLAND, WILLIAM, '46.
  Died December 20, 1880.
HOWLAND, WILLIAM WARE, REV., '41.
  Oodoville, Tappia, Ceylon.
HOYT, JAMES HUMPHREY, LL.B., '73.
  105 Public Square, Cleveland, Ohio.
HUMPHREY, HENRY MARTYN, '42.
  Died July 4, 1841.
HUMPHREY, LEONARD, '46.
  Died November 30, 1850.
HUMPHREY, ZEPHANIAH MOORE, REV., '43.
  Died November 12, 1881.
HUNT, JOHN SAVAGE, '87.
  Utica, N. Y.
HUNTINGTON, ELLERY CHANNING, '88.
  Amherst College, Amherst, Mass.
HUNTINGTON, FREDERIC DAN, RT. REV., '39.
  Syracuse, N. Y.

HUNTTING, SAMUEL, REV., '44.
　　Died September 10, 1849.
HUTCHINSON, HENRY ELIJAH, '58.
　　1346 Pacific St., Brooklyn, N. Y.
HUTCHINSON, HORACE, REV., '39.
　　Died March 7, 1846.
HUTCHINSON, PROPER KIMBALL, M.D., '41.
　　Died November 1, 1872.
HYDE, GEORGE MERRIAM, '88.
　　Amherst College, Amherst, Mass.
IRWIN, DAVID ALBION, '64.
　　Ret. Captain U. S. Army, Zellwood, Fla.
JAMES, ARTHUR CURTISS, '89.
　　Amherst College, Amherst, Mass.
JEWETT, GEORGE BAKER, REV., '40.
　　Died June 9, 1886.
KELLY, ARTHUR WILLARD, REV., '79.
　　Auburndale, Mass.
KELLY, EDWARD PARKER, '90.
　　Amherst College, Amherst, Mass.
KELSEY, HENRY SYLVESTER, REV., '55.
　　499 La Salle Ave., Chicago, Ill.
KEMP, JAMES FURMAN, '81.
　　443 Washington Ave., Brooklyn, N. Y.
KIDDER, WILLIAM MAGEE, '87.
　　18 Wall St., New York City.
KIMBALL, DAVID MATHER, '44.
　　Died October 23, 1857.
KIMBALL, FRANK FARNUM, '76.
　　215 Ryerson St., Brooklyn, N. Y.
KIMBALL, JOSEPH, '57.
　　Andover, Mass.
KNAPP, GEORGE SPENCER, '71.
　　267 Wabash Ave., Chicago, Ill.
KYBURG, GEORGE WILSON, '90.
　　Amherst College, Amherst, Mass.
LADD, CHARLES ELLIOTT, '81.
　　Portland, Oregon.
LADD, WILLIAM MEAD, '78.
　　Portland, Oregon.

LAMB, WILLIAM GEORGE, '85.
    South Hadley Falls, Mass.
LANE, CHARLES STODDARD, REV., '80.
    Unionville, Conn.
LANE, JAMES PILLSBURY, REV., '57.
    Norton, Bristol Co., Mass.
LARNED, STEPHEN HOLMES, '69.
    74 Lincoln St., Worcester, Mass.
LEARNED, SAMUEL JULIUS, '45.
    Lake Forest, Ill.
LELAND, GEORGE ADAMS, M.D., '74.
    349 Marlborough St., Boston, Mass.
LEWIS, FRANCIS DRAPER, LL.B., '69.
    411 Walnut St., Philadelphia, Pa.
LEWIS, JAMES, REV., '61.
    205 N. Scott St., Joliet, Ill.
LEWIS, THOMAS AUGUSTUS, '59.
    Died July 9, 1865.
LEWIS, ZECHARIAH EDWARDS, M.D., '62.
    New Rochelle, N. Y.
LINDSAY, GEORGE WALTER, '86.
    Care of W. C. R. R., Waukesha, Wis.
LINNELL, JONATHAN EDWARDS, M.D., '44.
    Norwich, Conn.
LINNELL, NATHAN SEABURY, '43.
    Died September 10, 1843.
LIPPITT, ANDREW CLARK, JR., LL.B., '66.
    New London, Conn.
LITTLE, ARTHUR MITCHELL, '88.
    Amherst College, Amherst, Mass.
LITTLE, REV. GEORGE OBADIAH, '60.
    216 I St., N. W., Washington, D. C.
LITTLE, JOSEPH BREWSTER, REV., '60.
    224 East 12th St., Davenport, Iowa.
LIVERMORE, AARON RUSSELL, REV., '37.
    Fairhaven, Conn.
LORD, NATHAN LYNDS, REV., '37.
    Rochester, Fulton Co., Ind.
LORING, ROBERT PEARMAIN, M.D., '74.
    Newton Centre, Mass.

LYON, APPLETON PARK, '70.
180 Fifth Avenue, New York City.

LYON, WALTER HUNTINGTON, '51.
Died November 13, 1853.

MARBLE, CHARLES FRANCIS, '86.
7 Beaver St., Worcester, Mass.

MARCH, CHARLES AUGUSTUS, '70.
195 Lake St., Chicago, Ill.

MARCH, DANIEL, REV., '38.
Woburn, Mass.

MARCH, DANIEL, JR., M.D., '65.
Winchester, Mass.

MARCH, FRANCIS ANDREW, '45.
Lafayette College, Easton, Pa.

MARCH, FREDERIC WILLIAM, REV., '67.
Tripoli, Syria.

MARCY, ALEXANDER, M.D., '59.
Camden, N. J.

MARSH, FRANK BALLARD, '83.
79 Spring St., New York City.

MARSHALL, JONATHAN BRYANT, '38.
Died June 30, 1861.

MARTIN, EDWIN KONIGMACHER, '71.
Lancaster, Pa.

MATTHEWS, HENRY MARTYN, '69.
116 La Salle St., Chicago, Ill.

MAYNARD, EDWARD, '62.
Died January 10, 1868.

MAYNARD, HORACE, '38.
Knoxville, Knox Co., Tenn.

MAYNARD JAMES, '74.
1340 R St. N.W., Washington, D. C.

McELHINNEY, JOHN WILLIAM, LL.B., '72.
Clayton, St. Louis Co., Mo.

McGLATHERY, WILLIAM, REV., '62.
Middletown, N. Y.

McKINSTRY, JOHN ALEXANDER, REV., '38.
Richfield, Summit Co., Ohio.

McMANUS, PARKER WHITTLESEY, '63.
Davenport, Iowa.

MEARS, LEVERETT, '74.
　Williamstown, Mass.
MILLER, ALBERT BARNES, '70.
　Died June 7, 1871.
MILLER, JOHN HAMILTON, '88.
　Amherst College, Amherst, Mass.
MILLER, SAMUEL FISHER, '48.
　Died October 28, 1870.
MILLIKEN, ARTHUR NORRIS, LL.B., '80.
　15 Ashburton Place, Boston, Mass.
MILLS, CHARLES SMITH, REV., '82.
　Springfield, Vt.
MILLS, FRANK SMITH, '87.
　Andover, Mass.
MONTELIUS, WILLIAM PIPER, '63.
　Died June 16, 1865.
MONTGOMERY, ALEXANDER, REV., '37.
　Died February 25, 1859.
MORRIS, GEORGE BLISS, LL.B., '37.
　Died July 7, 1872.
MORSE, JASON, REV., '45.
　Died October 14, 1861.
MORSE, LEONARD, '71.
　Hartford, Conn.
MOSMAN, WALTER BEMIS, '78.
　26 Broadway, New York City.
NEILL, HEMAN HUMPHREY, REV., '66.
　Amherst, Mass.
NEWHALL, GEORGE HARRISON, REV., '45.
　Died August 24, 1853.
NEWLIN, ELLIS JAMES, REV., '41.
　Died December 12, 1886.
NORRIS, KINGSLEY FLAVEL, REV., '73.
　1336 Jefferson St., N. E., Minneapolis, Minn.
NORTHROP, EDWIN FITCH, '90.
　Amherst College, Amherst, Mass.
NORTHROP, HENRY DAVENPORT, REV., '57.
　831 North Broad St., Philadelphia, Pa.
NOYES, STEPHEN DUTTON, REV., '66.
　93 Fair St., Kingston, N. Y.

OSBORNE, THEODORE MOODY, '71.
  6 Carpenter St., Salem, Mass.
PACKARD, ABEL KINGMAN, REV., '45.
  Highland Lake, Col.
PACKARD, FRANK EDWARDS, '80.
  Campello, Mass.
PAINE, ALBERT GEORGE, M.D., '72.
  3964 Drexel Boulevard, Chicago, Ill.
PAINE, CHARLES GOODELL GODDARD, '61.
  22 Selden Ave., Detroit, Mich.
PAINE, LYMAN MAY, '72.
  175 Dearborn St., Chicago, Ill.
PALMER, JAMES HENRY, '57.
  Died
PARK, CHARLES WARE, REV., '67.
  Birmingham, Conn.
PARK, EBENEZER BURGESS, '64.
  Osaya Mission, Kansas.
PARSONS, JOHN, REV., '73.
  1121 Seventeenth St., Denver, Col.
PAULLIN, HENRY, '76.
  Cherokee, Iowa.
PEASE, EDMUND MORRIS, M.D., REV., '54.
  Care Rev. A. O. Forbes, Honolulu, Hawaiian Isl.
PECKHAM, JOSEPH, REV., '37.
  Died May 17, 1884.
PECKHAM, WILLIAM CLARK, '67.
  Adelphi Academy, Brooklyn, N. Y.
PEPPER, GEORGE DANA BOARDMAN, REV., '57.
  Waterville, Me.
PERRY, JOSEPH HARTSHORN, '82.
  35 West St., Worcester, Mass.
PETTIBONE, BENJAMIN WELCH, '60.
  Winchester Centre, Conn.
PETTIBONE, IRA WELCH, '54.
  188 and 190 Washington St., Chicago, Ill.
PHELPS, AUSTIN, REV., '38.
  Andover, Mass.
PIERCE, EDWARD WILLARD, '59.
  Died September 13, 1871.

PLIMPTON, SALEM MARSH, REV., '46.
Died September 14, 1866.
PLUMMER, HENRY IRVING, '78.
Died December 30, 1874.
PRATT, CHARLES MILLARD, '79.
26 Broadway, New York City.
PRATT, CHARLES RANSOM, '69.
Elmira, N. Y.
PRATT, FRED. BAYLEY, '87,
232 Clinton Ave., Brooklyn, N. Y.
PRATT, GEORGE HARLOW, REV., '64.
Talcottville, Conn.
PRATT, THEODORE CONSTANTINE, REV., '57.
Auburn, N. H.
PRATT, WILLIAM ORRIN, '77.
The Pratt Institute, Ryerson St., Brooklyn, N. Y.
PRENTICE, EZRA PARMELEE, '85.
Room A, 55 Dearborn St., Chicago, Ill.
PRENTICE, PIERREPONT ISHAM, '90.
10 Tower Place, Chicago, Ill.
PRESTON, JAMES WILLARD, '39.
Longwood Avenue, Brookline, Mass.
PRICE, SAMUEL HARRISON, '39.
Lewisburgh, W. Va.
PRIEST, SYLVANUS CHICKERING, '58.
Died August 25, 1858.
RAE, ALEXANDER, M.D., '83.
21 Clinton St., Brooklyn, N. Y.
RAND, EDWARD GILLETT, '81.
466 Broad St., Providence, R. I.
REED, GEORGE MILTON, LL.B., '62.
246 Washington St., Boston, Mass.
REED, WILLIAM BARRETT, M.D., '37.
Died December 6, 1846.
REEVES, THOMAS, REV., '75.
Woonsocket, R. I.
RHEES, RUSH, '83.
Plainfield, N. J.
RICE, DANIEL, REV., '37.
Macalester College, Macalester, Minn.

RICE, STILLMAN, '56.
    Gloucester, Mass.
RICHARDS, JAMES AUSTIN, M.D., '51.
    Died June 4, 1859.
RICHARDSON, HENRY BULLARD, '69.
    Amherst, Mass.
RICHARDSON, JOHN KENDALL, '69.
    Newton, Mass.
ROBBINS, EDWARD COMBS, '63.
    3504 Lindell Ave., St. Louis, Mo.
ROCKWELL, FRANCIS WARREN, M.D., '65.
    6 Lafayette Ave., Brooklyn, N. Y.
ROCKWELL, FRANCIS WILLIAMS, LL.B., '68.
    Pittsfield, Mass.
ROCKWELL, JOEL EDSON, REV., '37.
    Died July 29, 1882.
ROCKWELL, ROBERT CAMPBELL, '71.
    Lenox, Mass.
ROOT, HENRY DWIGHT, '52.
    Died September 3, 1855.
ROWLAND, LYMAN SIBLEY, REV., '58.
    Lee, Mass.
SALTER, SUMNER, '77.
    15 Capitol Place, Atlanta, Ga.
SANDERS, ORREN BURNHAM, M.D., '78.
    376 Columbus Ave, Boston, Mass.
SANFORD, ABBOTT, '77.
    Everett, Mass.
SANFORD, BAALIS, '45.
    Died   , 1875.
SANFORD, ELLIOT, LL.B., '61.
    95 Nassau St. New York City.
SANFORD, JOHN ELIOT, '51.
    Taunton, Mass.
SARGENT, WILLIAM ARTHUR, LL.B., '79.
    39 Equitable Building, Boston, Mass.
SAVILLE, HENRY MARTYN, M.D., '54.
    Died January 11, 1881.
SAWYER, JOSEPH HENRY, '65.
    Easthampton, Mass.

SAYLOR, FRANCIS HOFFMAN, '65.
   257 South 4th St., Philadelphia, Pa.
SCOVILLE, FRANK CHURCHILL, REV., '75.
   Greenwich, N. Y.
SESSIONS, ROBERT HARVEY, '88.
   Amherst College, Amherst, Mass.
SHATTUCK, ELIJAH CARTER, '50.
   Berlin, Worcester Co., Mass.
SHEPARD, EDWARD OLCOTT, '60.
   37 Equitable Building, Boston, Mass.
SHEPARD, LUTHER DIMMICK, D.D.S., '62.
   100 Boylston St., Boston, Mass.
SHEPARDSON, DANIEL, REV., '39.
   Granville, Ohio.
SIEBERT, CHARLES ALBERT, '72.
   414 Olive St., St. Louis, Mo.
SKEELE, ARTHUR FESSENDEN, REV., '75.
   Augusta, Me.
SKEELE, WALTER FISHER, '88.
   Amherst College, Amherst, Mass.
SLEEPER, WILLIAM WASHBURN, REV., '78.
   Care of A. B. C. F. M., Boston, Mass.
SMART, ISAAC CHIPMAN, REV., '81.
   Pittsfield, Mass.
SMITH, BRYANT, '87.
   Milwaukee, Wis.
SMITH, BENJAMIN ELI, '77.
   The Century Co., 33 East 17th St., New York.
SMITH, BENTLEY HOWARD, '51.
   Joanna Furnace, Pa.
SMITH, CHARLES FULLER, '38.
   Died December 8, 1863.
SMITH, CURTIS BENJAMIN MINOR, '37.
   Died June 18, 1877.
SMITH, CHARLES SPRAGUE, '74.
   Columbia College, New York City.
SMITH, EDWARD ROBINSON, '76.
   1227 Broadway, New York City.
SMITH, HORACE PAYSON, REV., '54.
   Died March 12, 1877.

SMITH, THEODORE, '86.
  Cimarron, New Mexico.
SMITH, THOMAS SNELL, REV., '66.
  Tillipally, Jaffna, Ceylon.
SMITH, VINCENT HENRY, '42.
  Died August 29, 1868.
SPAULDING, SAMUEL THOMSON, '39.
  Died October 7, 1877.
SPAULDING, TIMOTHY GRIDLEY, '72.
  Northampton, Mass.
SPENCER, JOHN LAURENS, '48.
  Died October 12, 1851.
SPOFFORD, HENRY MARTYN, '40.
  Died August 20, 1880.
SPROUT, WILLIAM BRADFORD, '83.
  Room 119, 405 Main St., Worcester, Mass.
STANTON, GEORGE FRANCIS, REV., '63.
  21 Congregational House, Boston, Mass.
STEBBINS, FRANK EDWARD, '80.
  U. S. Patent Office, Washington, D. C.
STEBBINS, MILAN CYRUS, REV., '51.
  Cornwall, Vt.
STEVENS, HENRY AUGUSTUS, REV., '57.
  Bristol, R. I.
STILES, FRANKLIN OSGOOD, '56.
  Died January 26, 1857.
STOCKBRIDGE, HENRY (SMITH), '45.
  313 St. Paul St., Baltimore, Md.
STOKES, HARRY SHELBY, LL.B., '71.
  Died January, 1875.
STOKES, JAMES FRAZER, LL.B., '67.
  Terrene, Bolivar Co., Miss.
STOKES, WILLIAM CAMPBELL, '69.
  Died February 2, 1869.
STONE, HENRY DWIGHT, '44.
  Died October 27, 1869.
STONE, TIMOTHY PORTER, '62.
  Died 1864.
STONE, WILLIAM PIERCE, '64.
  Died November 9, 1862.

STORRS, HENRY EDWARD, '64.
Jacksonville, Ill.
STORRS, HENRY MARTYN, REV., '46.
Orange, N. J.
STORRS, RICHARD SALTER, REV., '39.
80 Pierrepont St., Brooklyn, N. Y.
STORRS, RICHARD SALTER, '53.
Died
STOWE, TIMOTHY, REV., '47.
Died August 11, 1866.
SUMNER, GEORGE, JR., '39.
Died October 29, 1852.
SYBRANDT, WILLIAM HENRY, REV., '76.
14th St., Troy, N. Y.
TAYLOR, HORACE WILLARD, '48.
Rockford, Ill.
TEAD, EDWARD SAMPSON, '75.
Somerville, Mass.
TENNEY, ALBERT FRANCIS, '69.
Madison, N. J.
THAYER, JAMES SMITH, '38.
Died January 19, 1881.
THOMPSON, ALBERT HENRY, REV., '72.
Wakefield, N. H.
THOMPSON, AMHERST LORD, REV., '51.
Died August 25, 1860.
THOMPSON, FREDERIC MINER, '87.
175 Herkimer St., Brooklyn, N. Y.
THOMPSON, JOHN HOWLAND, '50.
81 Clark St., Chicago, Ill.
THRESHER, ALMON UNDERWOOD, '65.
Granville, Ohio.
THURSTON, HIRAM EDWARD, '79.
Box 626, Providence, R. I.
THURSTON, THATCHER THAYER, '81.
Fall River, Mass.
TITUS, JOSEPH AUGUSTUS, '63.
Worcester, Mass.
TOBEY, RUFUS BABCOCK, REV., 77.
Ashburnham, Mass.

TOMSON, TRUMAN, '62.
  Died November 7, 1866.
TORREY, DAVID, REV., '43.
  Cazenovia, N. Y.
TOWER, FRANCIS EMORY, REV., '60.
  Bristol, Conn.
TOWNE, EDWARD SOUTHWORTH, REV., '64.
  Vineland, N. J.
TRAIN, GORHAM, '52.
  Northampton, Mass.
TREADWAY, ALLEN TOWNER, '86.
  Stockbridge, Mass.
TUCKER, EDWIN BENJAMIN, '85.
  358 West 30th St., New York City.
UNDERHILL, JOHN WINN, REV., '54.
  Died October 17, 1862.
WACKERHAGEN, PHILIP MAYER, '81.
  756 Broadway, Albany, N. Y.
WADHAMS, RALPH HOLBERTON, '89.
  Amherst College, Amherst, Mass.
WAITE, GEORGE WHITE, '61.
  Oberlin, Ohio.
WALKER, WILLISTON, '83.
  Emilien Strass, 13, Leipzig, Germany.
WARD, JAMES WILSON, REV., '26.
  Died February, 1, 1873.
WARD, JAMES WILSON, JR., REV., '60.
  Died October 30, 1875.
WARD, JOHN LORD HAYES, '59.
  Died August 1, 1859.
WARD, WILLIAM HAYES, REV., '56.
  "The Independent," New York City.
WARNER, AARON EDWARDS, LL.B., '61.
  Died
WARREN, FREDERICK MORRIS, '80.
  Johns Hopkins University, Baltimore, Md.
WASHBURN, CHARLES ELLERY, M.D., '38.
  Died April 10, 1865.
WASHBURN, WILLIAM IVES, LL.B., '76.
  3 Broad St., New York City.

WEEDEN, CHARLES FOSTER, '84.
   Hosmer Hall, Hartford, Conn.
WEEDEN, WILLIAM ORNE, REV., '77.
   Care of Clinton R. Weeden, Providence, R. I.
WELLMAN, ARTHUR HOLBROOK, LL.B., '78.
   24 Congress St., Boston, Mass.
WELLS, GEORGE HUNTINGTON, REV., '63.
   Montreal, Can.
WELLS, WILLIAM HARVEY, '36.
   Died January 21, 1885.
WHEELER, WILLARD HAYDEN, '84.
   274 Washington Ave., Brooklyn, N. Y.
WHIPPLE, WILLIAM WARD, REV., '41.
   Camp Point, Ill.
WHITE, WILLIAM PRESCOTT, REV., '67.
   Germantown, Philadelphia, Pa.
WHITING, WILLIAM HAMMOND, '64.
   Died December 29, 1874.
WHITNEY, HARRY MARTIN, JR., '78.
   Honolulu, Hawaiian Islands.
WILDER, JOSEPH EELLS, '63.
   Died April 8, 1864.
WILDER, WILLIAM FRANKLIN, '56.
   Colorado Springs, Col.
WILLARD, THOMAS CLIFTON, '87.
   814 Boltwood Ave., Cleveland, Ohio.
WILLIAMS, ELIJAH HAWLEY, '73.
   Springfield, Mo.
WILLIAMS, GEORGE HUNTINGTON, Ph.D. '78.
   John Hopkins University, Baltimore, Md.
WILLIAMS, HORACE ROBBINS, REV., '60.
   Clinton, Mich.
WILLIAMS, HENRY WARREN, '37.
   Died 1877.
WILLIAMS, HINCKLEY WRIGHT, '66.
   Died August 25, 1864.
WILLIAMS, JOHN CAMP, '82.
   Care of Crane Bros. Mfg. Co., Chicago, Ill.
WILLIAMS, JOHN HEALY, REV., '68.
   2008 East Seventh St., Kansas City, Mo.

WILLIAMS, STALHAM LEON, JR., '90.
Amherst College, Amherst, Mass.
WILLIAMS, TALCOTT, '73.
Philadelphia "Press," Philadelphia, Pa.
WILLIAMS, WILLIAM HERBERT, '76.
Springfield, Mo.
WILSON, ANDREW, REV., '42.
Died February 27, 1878.
WILSON, PETER HOWARD, '89.
Amherst College, Amherst, Mass.
WILSON, THADDEUS, REV., '43.
Shrewsbury, N. J.
WITHINGTON, NATHAN NOYES, '51.
Newburyport, Mass.
WITHINGTON, WILLIAM SHERBURNE, '41.
Died May 20, 1841.
WOOD, HOWARD OGDEN, '80.
80 St. Mark's Place, Brooklyn, N. Y.
WOOD, IRA COUCH, '86.
Oak Park, Cook Co, Ill.
WOOD, ISAAC WILLARD, LL.B., '68.
Grand Rapids, Mich.
WOOD, WALTER CHILDS, '86.
19 Argyle Place, Edinburgh, Scotland.
Care of Brown, Shipley & Co, London, England.
WOODBRIDGE, FREDERICK JAMES EUGENE, '89. Amherst College, Amherst, Mass.
WOODBRIDGE, JOHN, '49.
80 Dearborn St., Chicago, Ill.
WOODBRIDGE, JOHN, JR., '73.
80 Dearborn St., Chicago, Ill.
WOODMAN, GEORGE SULLIVAN, M.D., '46.
Newtonville, Mass.
WRIGHT, CHARLES HANDEL, '78.
40 West Broadway, New York City.
WRIGHT, RUSSELL MEDAD, '44.
Castleton, Rutland Co., Vt.
WYMAN, HENRY NEHEMIAH, LL.B., '45.
San Francisco, Cal.
WYMAN, WALTER, M.D., '70.
U. S. Marine Hospital Service, Battery, New York.
YOE, LUCIEN GURNEE, '68.
43 River St., Chicago, Ill.

www.ingramcontent.com/pod-product-compliance
Lightning Source LLC
Chambersburg PA
CBHW020258170426

43202CB00008B/428